*The social life of a household centers about its
dining-table, and every accessory that builds the
table-picture furthers the art of gracious living.
This illustration shows one cover correctly set, in
the dining-room of the Delineator Home Institute*

NEW
DELINEATOR
RECIPES

●

INCLUDING

TEN EXCLUSIVE
RECIPES

by

ANN BATCHELDER
DELINEATOR HOME INSTITUTE

Printed in the United States of America by
THE JOHN F. CUNEO COMPANY, CHICAGO

CONTENTS

FOOD FACTS YOU SHOULD KNOW

MEASUREMENTS AND EQUIVALENTS

Learn to Measure Accurately.—All the measurements in this book and in most standard cook-books and magazines are level. It will not do to use a heaping teaspoonful, tablespoonful or cupful when a level one is meant. To change proportions by wrong measuring causes poor results, for example:

Too much flour will make a cake dry and crumbly, bread solid and heavy, sauces thick and pasty.

Too much fat will make cakes oily and may cause them to fall. It will make grease-soaked doughnuts and greasy gravies and sauces.

Too much sugar will make a cake with a hard crust, or a sticky cake. It makes a soft, sticky jelly.

Too much liquid will make a cake that falls easily.

Too much soda gives a disagreeable taste and bad color to breads and cakes.

All recipes in this book are designed for six portions unless otherwise specifically stated.

DIRECTIONS FOR FRYING

1. Put enough fat into the kettle to submerge to a depth of one or two inches the articles to be fried. Do not fill kettle more than three-fourths full of fat. The fat in an over-full kettle may bubble over and catch fire.

2. Heat fat gradually to the desired temperature, which will be between 300° and 400° Fahrenheit, or always, if possible, below the smoking point of the fat.

3. Put only moderate amounts of food into the fat at one time, because (a) when the very hot fat cooks the food it causes the moisture in the food to boil and this vigorous bubbling may cause the fat to bubble over the edge of the kettle, with risk of fire; and (b) too much food may so cool the fat as to delay the cooking and increase absorption of fat and make a greasy product.

4. When the food is cooked to the desired brown color, remove at once, drain over the fat kettle for a few seconds, then place on soft paper to finish draining.

5. After frying is completed, let fat cool until it is safe to handle, then strain through several thicknesses of cheese-cloth placed over a strainer. Clarify it frequently, after each time of using, if possible, as it will lengthen the lifetime of the fat.

If fat used in frying is not overheated, and if it is frequently clarified, it may be used over and over again, even if the smoking temperature is comparatively low.

If fish is well egged and crumbed before being fried, it will not seriously flavor the fat in which it is fried and the fat is then useful for frying foods other than fish.

TESTING FAT FOR FRYING

Meat, Poultry, Fish
Temperature of fat—375°—390° F.
A cube of bread will brown in 40 to 50 seconds.

Vegetables
French Fried Potatoes, Onions, etc., 395° F.
A cube of bread will brown in 40 to 50 seconds.

Doughnuts—Fritters
All uncooked batter and dough mixtures—360°—370° F.
A cube of bread will brown in 60 seconds.

EGGING AND CRUMBING FOODS FOR FRYING

Except in the case of foods like doughnuts, fritters, potatoes and fried breads, foods are ordinarily either egged and crumbed or dipped in an egg batter before being fried. This is because the egg or egg batter hardens in the hot fat, making a case about the food which keeps it from becoming fat-soaked.

For crumbing, use dried bread crumbs rolled and sifted or soft crumbs forced through a strainer.

Break an egg into a shallow plate and beat it with a fork only enough to mix the yolk and white and not enough to beat air into it. Blend into the mixed egg two tablespoons water for each egg.

Place some crumbs on a board. Roll the food to be fried in the crumbs, covering all parts with crumbs.

Dip the crumb-covered food into the egg bath, being careful to cover every part with egg.

Lift food from egg with broad-bladed knife and roll again in crumbs.

Let stand a few moments to dry. The food is then ready for frying. Foods may be egged and crumbed several hours or even a day before being fried.

WHY CUSTARDS WHEY OR CURDLE

Custards usually whey or separate or curdle because they are cooked at too high a temperature. Soft custards may curdle when they are cooked for too long a time or are not stirred constantly. Milk that is a little sour may cause curdling of a custard.

The best way to prevent wheying, separating or curdling is to regulate the temperature and time of cooking all custards by cooking them over or surrounded by water slightly below the boiling-point, by removing them from the heat when they are done, and by being sure that milk used in making them is entirely sweet.

If a soft custard begins to whey, separate, or, as it is usually called in this case, curdle, it should be removed immediately from the heat. The pan containing it may be set in a pan of cold water, and the custard may be beaten vigorously to redistribute the particles of egg and milk solids.

DIRECTIONS FOR MIXING CUSTARDS

Scald the liquid. This saves time in making all custards.

Thoroughly mix eggs, seasoning (as salt), and flavoring (as sugar) by stirring but not by beating.

Gradually add hot liquid to egg mixture.

For **firm** custards, pour custard mixture into baking-dish, set baking-dish in pan of hot water and cook in oven or steamer until firm, keeping water in pan constantly below the boiling-point. The custard is done when the blade of a knife run into the center of the custard comes out clean.

For **soft** custards, cook in top of double boiler, keeping the water in the lower part constantly just below the boiling-point. Stir constantly until the mixture stops frothing, coats the spoon, and has the thickness of cream. Remove at once.

Latticed cucumbers, pineapple wedges and lettuce, served with cheese toast. Lobster, tomato and bacon salad with mayonnaise. Jellied fruit salad with whipped cream dressing.

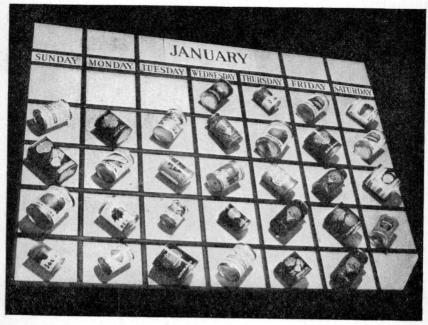

Canned vegetables provide a splendid variety for every day in the year.

Variety in the service of vegetables is always possible. For instance, here are three ways of serving asparagus hot.

SIMPLE MENUS

BREAKFASTS

Strawberries with Cream
Corn Flakes   Graham Muffins
Coffee   Milk

———

Stewed Apricots
Corn-Meal Mush   Buttered Toast
Coffee   Milk

———

Granular Wheat with Raisins and Top Milk
Oatmeal Gems   Eggs
Coffee   Milk

———

Baked Pears
French Toast   Maple Sirup
Coffee   Milk

———

Sliced Oranges
Scrambled Eggs and Bacon   Toast
Coffee   Milk

———

Grapefruit
Codfish Balls   Baking-Powder Biscuits
Coffee   Milk

———

Any Fruit in Season
Ham Omelet   Graham Biscuits
Coffee   Milk

———

Hot Baked Apples
Sausage Cakes   Popovers
Coffee   Milk

Oatmeal and Prunes with Top Milk
Corn Muffins   Boiled Eggs
Coffee   Milk

———

Oatmeal with Top Milk
or Bacon and Eggs
Toast   Marmalade
Coffee   Milk

———

Ready-to-Eat Cereal
Sliced Bananas with Top Milk
Poached Eggs on Toast   Toast
Coffee   Milk

LUNCHEONS OR SUPPERS

Banana and Nut Salad
Muffins   Honey
Milk   Tea

———

Spaghetti with Tomato Sauce
Waldorf Salad
Brown Bread Sandwiches
Milk   Tea

———

Delmonico Potatoes   Corn Oysters
Canned Fruit   Molasses Cookies

———

Cream of Potato Soup   Wafers
Asparagus Salad
Toast   Apple Jelly
Cocoa

———

Cream of Tomato Soup   Saltines
Apple and Celery Salad   Rolls

Creamed Salmon on Toast
Graham Bread and Butter
Sliced Oranges with Cocoanut

———

Cream of Potato Soup
Toasted Cheese Sandwiches
Fresh Fruit

———

Potato Salad   Sausages or Cold Ham
Apple Sauce   Biscuits

———

Lima Beans in Casserole   Muffins
Grapefruit and Celery Salad
Tea   Milk

———

Cream of Tomato Soup   Croutons
Brown Bread Sandwiches with Cheese Filling
Fruit Salad
Tea   Milk

———

Macaroni and Cheese
Stewed Tomatoes   Bread
Baked Apple with Tapioca
Tea   Milk

———

Pork and Beans
Pickle, Celery and Lettuce Salad
Brown Bread   Plum Sauce
Tea   Milk

———

Cabbage au Gratin   Plain Sandwiches
Lettuce Salad with French Dressing
Apricot and Rice Pudding

———

Cheese Soufflé   Baked Potatoes
Waldorf Salad   Rolls
Cocoa

Scalloped Oysters
Toasted English Muffins
Canned or Fresh Fruit
Tea   Milk

Creamed Salmon   Baked Potatoes
Pickles   Bread
Orange and Bermuda Onion Salad
Tea   Milk

Cold Meat   Tomato and Celery Salad
Hot Gingerbread and Whipped Cream
Bread
Tea   Milk

Cheese Fondue   Vegetable Salad
Bread
Cereal Pudding with Dates

Grapefruit
Tunafish Salad
French Fried Potatoes   Graham Gems
Floating Island Custard

DINNERS

Broiled Steak
Mashed Potatoes   Asparagus Salad
Rolls   Butter   Grape Conserve
Chocolate Pudding

Hamburg Steak with Tomato Sauce
Potato Cakes   Creamed Cauliflower
Rolls   Butter
Cranberry Sauce   Cookies

Breaded Pork Chops   Gravy
Riced Potatoes   Buttered Spinach
Combination Fruit Salad
Bread   Wafers

Liver and Bacon   Creamed Potatoes
Cabbage and Celery Salad
Bread
Sliced Bananas with Lemon-Juice

Veal Cutlets in Casserole
Creamed Potatoes   Eggplant
Watercress Salad
Apple Pie   Cheese   Coffee

———

Stuffed Beef Heart
Glazed Sweet Potatoes   Buttered Turnips
Cole-slaw
Tapioca Cream   Coffee

———

Clear Vegetable Soup
Roast Chicken   Giblet Gravy
Boiled Rice   Wax Beans
Asparagus Salad
Fruit Gelatin   Coffee

———

Pot Roast in Tomato Sauce   Potatoes
Buttered Peas   Brown Bread
Fresh Vegetable Salad
Fruit Jelly with Custard Sauce
Grapefruit
Broiled Steak   Potatoes on the Half Shell
Spinach   Hot Rolls
Molded Chocolate Pudding with Whipped Cream

———

Roast Mutton   Brown Gravy
Creamed Turnips   Mashed Potatoes
Currant Jelly   Bread
Lemon Sponge with Custard Sauce
Coffee

———

Roast Beef   Brown Gravy
Mustard or Horseradish Sauce
Franconia Potatoes   Fried Parsnips
Pumpkin Pie spread with Plum Jam
and Whipped Cream

Roast Pork   Brown Gravy
Apple Sauce or Small Baked Apples
Glazed Sweet Potatoes   Spinach
Macedoine of Fruit with Whipped Cream
Sponge Cakes

———

Pork Chops Baked with Apples
Scalloped Potatoes
String Beans   Bread
Indian Pudding

———

Swiss Steak   Baked Potatoes
Creamed Onions
Caramel Junket   Cookies

———

Meat Loaf   Scalloped Potatoes
Peas   Nut Bread
Lettuce Salad, Thousand Island Dressing
Fresh or Canned Fruit   Small Cakes

———

Fish Chowder with Water Wafers
Grapefruit Salad
Graham Bread and Butter
Queen of Puddings

———

Broiled Chicken   Riced Potatoes
Corn Fritters   Rolls
Tomato Jelly Salad
Apple Pie with Cheese

———

Meat Pie with Potatoes, Carrots and Turnips
Tomato Salad   Bread
Prune Whip   Custard Sauce

Tomato Soup   Bread Sticks
Baked Ham   Southern Sweet Potatoes
Green Peas   Rolls
Lettuce Salad   French Dressing
Meringues with Fruit and Whipped Cream
Coffee

———

Cream of Corn Soup
Baked Hash   Spinach with Egg
Chocolate Bread Pudding
Coffee

———

Salmon Loaf with Cream Peas
Mashed Potatoes
Apple and Celery Salad
Banana Cream Pie

———

Broiled Halibut   Creamed Potatoes
Chili Sauce
Cole-slaw   Brown Bread
Rice Custard

———

Fruit Cocktail
Stuffed Turbans of Flounders
French Fried Potatoes
Creamed Peas   Bread or Rolls
Tomato Salad
Fruit Ice   Cakes   Coffee

TEN EXCLUSIVE RECIPES
By
ANN BATCHELDER

ORANGE AND SHRIMP SALAD

1 cup walnut meats, broken in pieces
6 oranges peeled and cut in sections
1 can shrimps
2 tablespoons cooking wine

Mix all in a stiff mayonnaise and serve chilled in orange cups or on crisp lettuce, and garnish with orange and thin slices of lemon.

CLAM FRITTERS

2 cups minced clams
2 eggs
½ cup milk
½ teaspoon salt

1 teaspoon grated horseradish
1¾ cups flour
1 teaspoon baking powder
Dash of cayenne

Beat eggs, add milk. Sift flour with seasonings and baking powder. Add milk and egg mixture to dry ingredients. Add horseradish. Stir clams into batter and drop by spoonfuls into hot fat and fry until brown. Drain. Serve hot with Chili Sauce.

MACARONI CROQUETTES

Cook one cup finely broken macaroni in boiling salted water about fifteen minutes. Make one cup thick white sauce, season with salt and pepper, add one-fourth cup grated cheese, beaten yolk of one egg. Mix all together, spread on platter to cool. Shape into croquettes, roll in crumbs, dip in beaten egg and crumbs again and fry in deep, hot fat. Drain and serve with cheese sauce.

16

SOPHIA SMITH PUDDING

½ cup sugar
¼ cup shortening
1 egg
½ cup milk

1 cup flour
2 teaspoons baking powder
1 teaspoon vanilla
A few grains of salt

Cream shortening, add sugar and egg, well beaten. Sift together flour, salt and baking powder. Add to mixture alternately with milk and beat well. Add vanilla. Bake in muffin tins in oven at 375° F. for ten to twelve minutes. Serve with rum sauce.

HOMESTEAD SAUCE

Beat 2 eggs until very light. Add ¾ cup sugar and beat. Add to 1 cup cream, whipped stiff, and flavor with 3 tablespoons rum extract. Serve on plum puddings or cottage pudding.

SPICE CAKE

1 cup shortening
3 cups brown sugar
3 eggs
1 cup chopped nuts
1 cup chopped raisins

3 cups flour
1 cup sour milk
1 teaspoon soda
1 teaspoon clove
1 teaspoon cinnamon

1 teaspoon nutmeg

Cream shortening, add sugar, beaten yolks of eggs. Sift flour with spices. Dissolve soda in sour milk. Add flour and milk alternately to mixture, beating well. Reserve one-half cup flour to dredge raisins. Add nuts and raisins and lastly the beaten whites. Bake in 3 layers in oven at 350°-375° F. for twenty-five to thirty minutes. Put layers together with jam and cover with white icing.

SPIDER CAKE

1 cup brown sugar
1 cup chopped nuts
4 teaspoons butter

1 cup chopped raisins
1 cup grated pineapple, thoroughly drained.

Melt butter in frying pan and add above ingredients, covering with the following batter:

½ cup shortening
1 cup sugar
2 cups flour
1 cup milk
1 teaspoon salt

1½ teaspoons baking powder
Yolks of 2 eggs
1 teaspoon lemon extract
Whites of 2 eggs, beaten stiff

Cream shortening, add sugar and yolks of eggs well beaten. Add flavoring. Add flour sifted with baking powder and salt, alternately with milk. Add stiffly beaten whites last. Bake in frying pan in oven at 350°-375° F. for about twenty to twenty-five minutes. When done turn upside down on plate. Serve hot or cold with sugar and cream.

CHOCOLATE ROLL

6 egg whites
⅓ cup sugar

⅓ cup cocoa
A few grains salt

Beat whites stiff, add salt, sugar and cocoa. Spread on cookie sheet, about eight inches wide, covering the sheet with greased paper. Bake at 300° F. for 15 to 20 minutes. Take out of oven, cover with whipped cream and roll as jelly roll. Put into refrigerator to chill. Slice.

SHREWSBURY CAKES

1 cup sugar
½ cup shortening
½ cup sour milk
A little nutmeg, mace

½ teaspoon soda
2 cups flour
¼ teaspoon salt
1 teaspoon lemon extract

Cream shortening, add sugar; dissolve soda in sour milk; sift flour with spices and salt. Add alternately with milk. Add extract. Drop in spoonsful on buttered sheet. Sprinkle with sugar and bake in oven at 275° F. for ten minutes.

SILVER LAKE HOUSE CREAM PIE

1 cup sugar
½ cup milk
2 teaspoons baking powder

1¼ cups flour
2 eggs
3 tablespoons melted butter

Sift flour, baking powder and sugar together. Add milk and beaten eggs and butter. Beat thoroughly. Bake in two layers in oven at 350°-375° F. for about fifteen minutes. Split layers and fill with custard as follows:

2 cups milk, 3 tablespoons sugar, 3 tablespoons corn starch, 1 egg, 2 teaspoons vanilla. Cook in double boiler until thick. Flavor and cool.

QUICK BREADS, GRIDDLE CAKES AND WAFFLES

POPOVERS

1¼ cups flour   1 teaspoon sugar
¼ teaspoon salt   1 cup milk
2 eggs

Mix the flour, salt and sugar. Gradually add the milk and the well-beaten eggs. Beat thoroughly. Have ready some small ramekins or iron muffin-pans, well greased and piping hot. Fill them about half full of the batter and bake in a hot oven for thirty to forty minutes. The heat should be reduced toward the end to prevent the popovers from becoming too brown.

BREAD-CRUM GRIDDLE-CAKES

1½ cups stale bread-crums   ½ cup flour
1½ cups scalded milk   ½ teaspoon salt
2 tablespoons shortening   4 teaspoons baking-powder
2 eggs

Soak the crums in the milk and fat until they are soft. Add the eggs, well beaten, and the dry ingredients, mixed and sifted. Drop the batter, by spoonfuls, on a hot, greased griddle. When the cakes are full of bubbles, turn them and brown on the other side. The cakes are very tender and should be turned carefully.

FRENCH OR JELLY PANCAKES

3 eggs   1 cup milk
1 teaspoon sugar   ½ cup flour
½ teaspoon salt   1 tablespoon shortening

Separate the yolks and whites of the eggs. To the beaten yolks add the sugar, salt and one-half cup of milk. Stir in the sifted flour, the other half cup of milk, the melted shortening, then fold in the stiffly beaten whites of the eggs. When eggs are high, use only two eggs and a half teaspoon of baking-powder.

19

Bake on a hot griddle, making the cakes slightly larger than usual. Spread each cake with tart fruit jelly and roll white hot. Place all on a platter, side by side, with the lapped edge of the roll touching the bottom of the platter to keep the cake from spreading. Dredge with sugar and, with a red-hot wire toaster, burn lines on the sugared pancakes. This gives an attractive appearance and a slight flavor of burnt sugar.

APPLE PANCAKES

1 tablespoon fat	1 teaspoon baking-powder
1 tablespoon sugar	1 cup apples
2 eggs	Cinnamon
1½ cups flour	Milk

Cream the fat and sugar, add the beaten eggs, the flour sifted with the baking-powder and cinnamon, and the finely chopped apples. Then gradually add milk to make a medium batter. Bake on a griddle as for ordinary pancakes and serve in an overlapping row around a platter of pork chops or serve separately with roast pork, either hot or cold. Cooked apples or a dry apple sauce may be used with batter in the same way.

WAFFLES

1½ cups flour	1 cup milk
½ teaspoon salt	2 eggs
3 teaspoons baking-powder	1 tablespoon fat

Mix the flour, salt and baking-powder, add the milk gradually, then the eggs, which have been beaten until very light, and the melted fat. Be sure that both sides of the waffle-iron are hot and that it is well greased. After baking each waffle, heat the iron a minute before putting in batter for the next.

MUFFINS

2 cups flour	1 cup milk
½ teaspoon salt	1 egg
1 tablespoon sugar	2 tablespoons melted shorten-
4 teaspoons baking-powder	ing

Mix and sift the flour, salt, sugar and baking-powder. Add the milk gradually, the well-beaten egg and melted fat. Pour

Here are beverages for every meal and for all sorts of enter-taining.

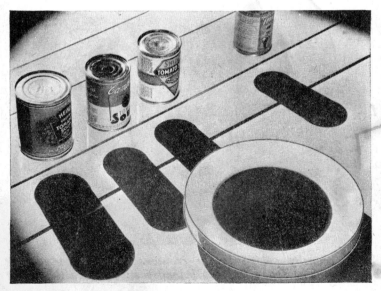

A delicious hot soup is always available at a moment's notice.

Evaporated milk may be used in any recipe which calls for milk. The well stocked pantry will contain a supply of this convenient product.

Crisp crunchy golden brown croutons garnish the cup of bouillon. The spoon and cup belong particularly to this soup.

into well-greased muffin-tins, filling the tins two-thirds full. Bake in a hot oven (400°-425° F.) from fifteen to twenty-five minutes.

GRAHAM MUFFINS

2 cups graham flour
2 tablespoons sugar
½ teaspoon salt
1 egg
½ teaspoon soda
¾ cup sour milk
½ tablespoon shortening

Sift the flour with the sugar, salt and soda, and turn the bran back into it. Add the milk gradually, the well-beaten egg, and the melted shortening. Fill well-greased muffin-tins about two-thirds full and bake in a hot oven (400°-425° F.) from twenty to twenty-five minutes.

CORN-MEAL MUFFINS

1 cup corn-meal
1 cup flour
½ teaspoon salt
4 teaspoons baking-powder
1 cup milk
1 egg
2 tablespoons shortening

Mix and sift the corn-meal, flour, salt and baking-powder. Add the milk gradually, then the well-beaten egg, and melted fat. Bake in well-greased muffin-pans in a hot oven (400°-425° F.).

JELLY CORN MUFFINS

Use the recipe for corn-meal muffins. Fill greased muffin-tins one-fourth full, put a teaspoon of jelly on the top of the batter in each cup, cover the jelly with more batter and bake in a hot oven (400°-425° F.) fifteen or twenty minutes.

BOSTON BROWN BREAD

1 cup corn-meal
1 cup rye flour
1 cup graham flour
¾ tablespoon soda
1 teaspoon salt
¾ cup molasses
2 cups sour milk or 1¾ cups
  sweet milk

Mix and sift the ingredients. Mix the molasses and milk and add to the dry ingredients. Beat thoroughly and turn into well-greased molds, filling each mold about two-thirds full. Cover and steam three hours. Remove the covers and bake the bread long enough to dry it off.

BAKING-POWDER BISCUITS

2 cups flour
4 teaspoons baking-powder
1 teaspoon salt

2 tablespoons shortening
¾ cup liquid (all milk or half
milk and half water)

Mix dry ingredients and sift twice. Work in fat with tips of the fingers, or cut in with two knives. Add the liquid gradually, mixing with a knife to a soft dough. Owing to differences in flours, it is impossible to determine the exact amount of liquid. Toss on a floured board, pat and roll lightly to one-half inch in thickness. Shape with a biscuit-cutter. Bake in hot oven (450°-460° F.) twelve to fifteen minutes.

EMERGENCY BISCUIT

Use the recipe for baking-powder biscuit, using more liquid to make the dough soft enough to drop from the spoon. The amount of the liquid in this recipe, in most cases, will be just half the amount of flour (two cups of flour to one cup liquid). Drop the biscuit on to a well-greased pan, or bake in greased muffin-tins, in a hot oven (450°-460° F.).

SALLY LUNN

½ cup shortening
¼ cup sugar
2 teaspoons baking-powder

2 cups flour
1 cup milk
1 egg

Cream the shortening with the sugar. Mix and sift together the flour and baking-powder and add to the creamed mixture, alternating with the milk. Add the beaten egg and bake in a loaf or in muffin-pans, in a moderate oven (350°-400° F.).

When fresh huckleberries are in season, one cup stirred in just before baking will be an agreeable addition.

ENGLISH MUFFINS

1 cup corn meal
1 cup flour
3 tablespoons sugar
4 teaspoons baking powder
1 teaspoon salt

1¼ cups milk
2 eggs
3 tablespoons melted shortening

Mix dry ingredients. Beat the eggs, add to milk with melted shortening. Combine mixtures. Pour into greased tin and bake in a moderate oven (325°-350° F.) for about thirty minutes.

CLOVER LEAF ROLLS

1½ cups scalded milk
3 yeast cakes
⅓ cup shortening
2 tablespoons sugar

1 teaspoon salt
1 whole egg
Flour to make a fairly stiff
  dough

Add sugar, salt and shortening to scalded milk and cool to lukewarm temperature. Dissolve yeast in one-half cup lukewarm
water and add to milk. Beat egg thoroughly and add. Mix in
flour to make a stiff dough. Cover and set in warm place to rise.
When risen to twice the bulk, take out on board, mold, form into
rolls of any desired shape, put into pans, let rise again to twice
the bulk, and bake in a quick oven (375°-400° F.) for about ten
minutes. Brush over with melted butter.

These rolls may be made up into clover leaves, Parker House,
braided or knotted rolls, bread sticks or cinnamon buns, all with
equal success. The whole process for these rolls requires only
from two to three hours.

To reheat these, or any other hot bread, never sprinkle with
water before heating, but simply put them on a baking sheet,
cover tightly with a cake tin, and heat in a moderate oven
(350° F.) for ten or fifteen minutes.

SWEDISH TEA RING

1 cup scalded milk
¾ teaspoon salt
¼ cup sugar
6 tablespoons shortening
⅛ cup finely chopped nuts

1 yeast cake softened in ¼ cup
  warm water
3½ cups flour
1 egg

Add the scalded milk to the salt, sugar and fat. When lukewarm add the yeast. Add one-half the flour and beat well. Let
rise until very light. When light add the egg and the remaining
flour and beat well. Let rise. Divide the dough into two parts

and shape each in a long, round piece and form two circles, plac·
ing the circles on a baking-tin. Brush with white of egg and
sprinkle with finely chopped nuts. With a large pair of scissors
cut toward the center of the ring, but not quite to the center, at
intervals of two inches, placing the cut section each time flat on
the tin, giving it a petal-like appearance. When light, bake in a
moderate oven (350°-400° F.).

COFFEE CAKE

1 cup scalded milk
¾ teaspoon salt
⅔ cup sugar
4 tablespoons shortening

1 cake yeast softened in ¼ cup
  warm water
1 egg
2 cups flour (about)
Sugar, cinnamon

Cool the milk and add the yeast and one-half the flour. Beat
well and let rise until very light. Add the slightly beaten egg,
sugar and melted fat, mix thoroughly and add remaining flour.
Let rise until almost double in bulk. Pour into shallow, greased
pans. When light, sprinkle thickly with sugar and cinnamon.
Bake twenty minutes at 400° F. Serve hot.

TOAST MELBA

Cut bread in one-eighth-inch slices and toast until crisp.

FRENCH TOAST

12 slices bread ½ inch thick
3 eggs
2 cups milk

½ teaspoon salt
Powdered sugar

Beat the eggs, add the milk and salt. Dip slices of bread into
this mixture and sauté in a little hot fat until a delicate brown.
Sprinkle with powdered sugar and serve hot.

USES FOR STALE BREAD

Stale bread should never be thrown away. The soft part may
be grated and used for soft crums. The larger pieces of bread
may be used for toast, croutons or toast sticks. The drier pieces
may be dried very slowly in the oven and then grated or ground
for dry crums.

SANDWICHES AND SANDWICH FILLINGS

ANCHOVY BUTTER

Yolks of 4 hard-cooked eggs   ½ cup butter
4 boned anchovies   Paprika

Rub the yolks of the hard-cooked eggs to a smooth paste with the anchovies and butter and add paprika to taste.

PEANUT BUTTER AND FRUIT

¼ cup figs   ½ teaspoon salt
¼ cup raisins   ½ cup peanut butter
2 tablespoons light corn-sirup

Wash figs and raisins and put through a food-chopper. Add salt, peanut butter, lemon-juice and corn-sirup, and mix well.

PEANUT BUTTER AND BANANA

½ cup peanut butter   ½ cup banana pulp or 2
¼ cup cream or hot water   bananas
Lemon-juice

Mix the peanut butter with the cream until smooth and light in color, then combine with banana pulp and lemon-juice, or slice banana over layer of peanut butter on bread.

PEANUT BUTTER AND PICKLE

½ cup peanut butter   ¼ cup hot water
½ cup chopped pickle

Cream peanut butter and water together and add chopped pickle.

ANCHOVY AND CHEESE SANDWICHES—NO. 1

10 tablespoons Parmesan   10 slices toasted bread
  cheese   5 anchovies

Add to the Parmesan cheese the anchovy and rub to a paste. Spread between two very thin slices of toasted buttered bread.

CHEESE AND ORANGE MARMALADE SANDWICHES

½ cup cream cheese   ½ cup orange marmalade
¼ cup cream

Spread half the slices with seasoned cheese, softened with the cream and mixed with seasoning if desired, the other half with orange marmalade to which is added a little French mustard, and fit slices together.

RUSSIAN SANDWICHES

½ cup Neufchatel cheese   ¼ cup chopped pimiento
¼ cup chopped olives   ¼ cup mayonnaise
10 lettuce leaves

Spread thin slices of Boston brown bread, lightly buttered, with Neufchatel cheese, or any other cream cheese. Spread also an equal number of buttered slices with finely chopped olives and pimientos mixed with mayonnaise dressing. Press together in pairs with a crisp lettuce leaf between.

CHICKEN SANDWICHES

2 egg-yolks   Salt
1 teaspoon melted butter   Pepper
1 teaspoon lemon-juice   1 teaspoon stock
1 cup chicken

Cook the eggs thirty to forty-five minutes, in water just below boiling-point, take out the yolks, and mash as fine as possible. Add to these the melted butter and lemon-juice, the finely chopped chicken, salt, pepper and stock. Mix all well together. A paste will be the result and with this very delicate sandwiches may be made.

LIVER AND BACON SANDWICHES

½ cup chopped bacon   ½ cup mashed liver
¼ cup cream   Salt and pepper

Mix chopped bacon and mashed liver, season with pepper and salt, and mix with cream. Decorate the plate with a border of lemon slices and hard-boiled eggs cut into halves lengthwise, with a sprig of cress or parsley on each.

Cereals, hot, dry, in so many stages of puffiness, flakiness, steaming goodness and crunchy tastiness, that every appetite under the sun is sure to be gratified, satisfied and perfectly content.

Toast, bacon, thinly sliced chicken, tomato and mayonnaise make the Club Sandwich, which is a meal in itself.

Sandwiches of many designs may be shaped with fancy cutters. For suggestions, see page 32.

Delicate sandwiches of infinite variety in materials, sizes and shapes, may be served with afternoon tea.

VARIATIONS FOR MEAT SANDWICHES

With corned beef or ham use a bit of mustard, with roast beef or tongue use Worcestershire or horseradish sauce. Chopped capers, tomato sauce, catchup or cold mint sauce are appropriate with lamb, and celery salt with veal. Onion-juice or finely chopped parsley adds a zest to any kind of fish or meat sandwiches.

FISH SANDWICHES

Anchovies, sardines, or freshly boiled fish may be used for sandwiches. These are better pounded to a paste, with a few drops of lemon-juice added during the pounding. Fresh white fish, like cod, may be seasoned with salt and pepper, moistened with a little mayonnaise or even a plain white sauce, and then put between two layers of buttered white bread.

OYSTER SANDWICHES

Place two or three fried oysters between two buttered slices of brown or white bread. They may be sprinkled with pepper, salt, horseradish, lemon-juice, tabasco, Worcestershire, or water-cress, according to taste.

RADISH SANDWICHES

½ cup potted ham   ½ cup sliced radishes
¼ to ½ cup mayonnaise

Peel and slice radishes, dip them in rich, thick mayonnaise, and lay on thin slices of bread covered with potted ham.

WHIPPED-CREAM SANDWICHES

½ cup cream   ½ cup chopped nuts
Powdered sugar   Vanilla

Whip cream very stiff. Add sugar to make it quite sweet, few drops of vanilla, and chopped nuts. Spread between very thin slices of buttered bread, and serve at once. Whipped cream mixed with pounded nut-meats, spread on buttered bread with candied fruits added, is delicious.

TWENTY SANDWICH SUGGESTIONS

1. Raisins worked into Neufchatel cheese.
2. Chopped raisins, figs, dates or prunes, and nut-meats moistened with mayonnaise dressing or lemon-juice.
3. The well-whipped white of an egg mixed with a cup each of chopped raisins and nut-meats, seasoned with a little salt.
4. Peanut butter moistened with salad dressing and mixed with raisins, dates, figs or bananas.
5. Equal parts olives, peanut butter, celery, mixed with a little salad dressing.
6. Peanut butter mixed with chopped dill, sweet or sour pickles.
7. Cream cheese and chopped stuffed olives.
8. Chopped stuffed olives and chopped nuts, moistened with salad dressing.
9. Cream cheese and shredded pineapple between very thin slices of bread.
10. Tunafish mixed with parsley, lemon-juice, seasoning and a bit of onion.
11. Cream cheese and chopped nuts.
12. Ground boiled ham and chopped pickles or chopped peanuts.
13. Cottage cheese and pickles, olives, nuts or pimientos.
14. Currant jam with pounded walnut meats and creamed butter. Pass with cream cheese. Preserved currants may be substituted in this combination.
15. Boston brown bread with cream cheese or mayonnaise and chopped nuts and raisins.
16. Rounds of brown bread spread with chopped olives, minced lettuce and watercress, tarragon, paprika, parsley and chives mixed with mayonnaise.
17. Pimientos, cucumbers and onion or chives, minced, mixed with mayonnaise and spread on buttered entire-wheat bread.
18. Green pepper, pimiento and olives with mayonnaise.
19. Boston brown bread with minced corned beef seasoned with mustard and rubbed to a paste.
20. Cream cheese used with chopped parsley, pimientos and mayonnaise, chopped nuts, sliced sugared bananas, chopped pineapples, chopped or sliced olives, shredded sliced apples. The cheese may be rubbed with butter or the creamed butter may be spread on the bread.

APPETIZERS

PREPARED BREAD FOR CANAPÉS

Canapés are made from stale white bread, cut in quarter-inch slices and then shaped with a cutter into circles or rings two and one-half or three inches in diameter or cut into squares, strips, triangles or other fancy shapes. These portions of bread are then either fried in deep fat and drained on absorbent paper or sautéd in just enough butter or other fat to keep them from burning; or they may be toasted.

ANCHOVY CANAPÉS

6 portions prepared bread   3 teaspoons lemon-juice
3 tablespoons anchovy paste   2 hard-cooked eggs
Garnish of whole anchovies (may be omitted)

Anchovies are small fish which are salted and preserved. Anchovy paste, which comes in tubes, jars or bottles, may be utilized, or whole anchovies may be reduced to a smooth paste with a wooden spoon. Season with lemon-juice and spread the paste on the prepared pieces of bread. Split two anchovies lengthwise and lay them diagonally across the canapé, marking the point where they cross by a little pyramid of riced yolk of hard-cooked eggs. Petal-shaped pieces of the hard-cooked white may radiate from this center pyramid. The anchovies may be omitted in the decoration. A large anchovy curved around a circle of hard-cooked egg in the center of a canapé is also effective.

SARDINE CANAPÉS

6 portions prepared bread   Worcestershire sauce
6 large sardines   Pickled beets
Juice of 1 lemon   6 large olives
Salt   24 thin slices lemon

Remove skin and backbone. Flake the sardines with a fork and season with lemon-juice, salt and a few drops of Worcestershire sauce. Spread the prepared bread with this mixture and decorate by placing in the center of each canapé a small circle of pickled beet. Cut a slice from the end of a large olive so that it will stand firmly and place this in the center of the beet. A narrow border of finely chopped beet may be placed around the edge of the canapé with good effect. Garnish the plate with four thin slices of lemon placed symmetrically.

CHEESE AND OLIVE CANAPÉS

6 portions prepared bread
3 tablespoons cream cheese
Olives stuffed with pimientos

Garnish of red pepper or
  pickled beet

Spread on the prepared bread a paste made by mixing equal proportions of cream cheese and chopped stuffed olives. Garnish with a quarter-inch border of the chopped olives and a star of red pepper or pickled beet in the center of each.

SUGGESTIONS FOR CANAPÉS

1. Spread rounds of bread, toasted and buttered, with purée of *pâté de foie gras*. On top of this place a slice of hard-boiled egg. Garnish with caviar and filet of anchovy.

2. Another way is to scoop the inside from small rolls, butter and toast them in the oven. Spread with purée of *foie gras* and return to the oven. When piping hot, fold in napkins and serve at once as first course.

3. Spread oblong pieces of bread buttered and toasted with sardine paste. Place a sardine on each and sprinkle with lemon-juice and chopped parsley. Or toast in the oven and serve hot with lemon.

4. Spread rounds of buttered bread with a paste made from finely chopped, hard-cooked egg. Decorate with a row of slices of gherkin. Or season caviar with lemon-juice and a dash of onion and garnish with a slice of olive.

5. Spread rounds of buttered toast with anchovy paste and then with a mixture of grated cheese and butter beaten to a cream. Reheat in the oven until the cheese melts. Garnish with a mushroom cap sautéd in fat or with a bit of watercress.

6. Spread rounds of buttered toast with anchovy paste and then with a mixture of shredded crab-meat mixed with cheese creamed with butter.

COCKTAILS WITH SHRIMPS

1. Shrimps may be put in glasses of cracked ice and each one dipped in mayonnaise. They may be served on glass plates.

2. Shrimps may be mashed in mayonnaise, put in green-pepper shells, garnished with red pepper and served with brown bread and butter.

STRAWBERRY-AND-PINEAPPLE COCKTAIL

1 cup orange-juice	Sugar
⅓ cup lemon-juice	1 cup strawberries
1 cup diced pineapple	

Combine the orange- and lemon-juice sweetened to taste, keeping the mixture rather tart. Place on ice. Wash and drain the strawberries and hull them. At serving time cut the berries into halves (except six large ones), mix them with the pineapple, place in glasses and cover with the fruit-juice. One large, perfect berry set on a tiny circle of pineapple may decorate the top of each cocktail.

MIXED FRUIT COCKTAIL

6 large oranges	Juice of 1 lemon
1 banana	Sugar
2 slices pineapple	

Slice off the tops of the oranges and scoop out the inside, being careful not to break the inside white skin of the orange-peel. Put the orange cups in a bowl of ice-water. Cut in small pieces the banana and pineapple, mix these with the orange pulp cut in small pieces and the lemon-juice, sweeten to taste, and then fill the orange shells. Set each one in a small bowl, filled with crushed ice. The mixed fruit pulp that remains after the orange skins have been filled may be kept in the refrigerator and served as sauce with ice-cream or used in any other way that circumstances suggest.

Fruit cocktails may be made from mixtures of almost any fruits, canned or fresh. As a rule, combinations of a sweet and a sour fruit are most piquant in flavor.

SOUPS

BAKED-BEAN SOUP

3 slices bacon
2 cups baked beans
4 cups cold water
1 tablespoon flour

1 tablespoon butter or butter
    substitute
Salt, pepper, paprika

Cook bacon. Add to beans. Add cold water and cook until beans are soft, then rub through a strainer. Place on the fire and add a little more water, if needed, as the soup must not be too thick. Bind with the flour and butter. Cook two or three minutes. Season with salt, a dash of pepper, and paprika.

CROŪTONS

Cut stale bread into slices about one-third of an inch thick, and remove all crust. Spread with butter, cut in cubes and bake in the oven until delicately browned. If preferred, these cubes of bread may be fried in deep fat or sautéd in just enough fat to keep them from burning. Put in soup at time of serving, or pass in a separate dish, permitting each person to put as many croutons as he may wish in his portion of soup.

ONION SOUP GRATINEE

3 onions
3 tablespoons butter
3 pints beef stock
3 tablespoons grated cheese

Pepper and salt
1/8 clove garlic (if desired)
2 tablespoons chopped parsley
1/4 loaf French bread

Slice onions and put them into a stew-pan with butter. Stir and fry slowly until softened and slightly browned. Add beef stock, boil ten minutes, skim, season, and add parsley and garlic. Cut the bread into thin slices, dry in the oven a few minutes, pour soup into a low earthen casserole, put bread on top, sprinkle with grated cheese, and set in a very hot oven just long enough to brown the cheese.

CREOLE SOUP

3 tablespoons green pepper chopped

2 tablespoons onion chopped

¼ cup savory fat

2 tablespoons flour

1 quart stock

1 pint tomatoes, fresh or canned

Salt and pepper

2 tablespoons grated horse-radish

1 teaspoon vinegar

Cook chopped green pepper and chopped onion in savory fat for five minutes. Add flour, stock, tomatoes, and simmer fifteen minutes. Rub through sieve and season with salt and pepper. Just before serving add grated horseradish and vinegar.

HOW TO PREVENT SKIN ON CREAM SOUPS

If a cream soup or a milk soup is beaten just before serving, the froth protects it against skin formation.

If a small portion of whipped cream or beaten egg-white is served on top of each portion of cream soup, it aids in preventing the skin formation as well as adds to the delicacy and attractiveness of the dish.

MUSHROOM SOUP

¼ pound mushrooms (or skin and stems of ½ pound)

2 tablespoons butter

2 tablespoons flour

1 teaspoon salt

1 pint milk

Brush, wash and skin the mushrooms. Put the skins to simmer in a little water. Cut the mushroom caps and stems into very small pieces; add one pint of water and simmer until tender. Make a sauce of the fat, flour, salt and milk and add the water in which the mushroom caps, stems and skin were cooked. The soup is more delicious if the diced caps and stems are added.

OYSTER STEW

1 pint oysters

4 tablespoons butter

Salt, pepper, paprika

1 quart rich milk

Put cleaned oysters, strained oyster liquor, butter, and seasoning into a saucepan and simmer gently until oysters curl at the edges. Add the milk and bring quickly to the simmering-point. Serve very hot.

GARNISHES

Garnishes should be simple, appropriate, easy to prepare, but they should not be used to disguise deficiencies or poor qualities of any dish. Edible garnishes are more appropriate than those that are used merely for appearance. At least one-third of a dish should be left free of garnish. The garnish should be so placed that it does not interfere with the service. With a few exceptions, such as candied or maraschino cherries, sweet pickles or preserved whole currants, strawberries or cranberries, sweets are not used to garnish savory dishes. Toast or puff pastes should not, as a rule, be used on the same dish with potatoes.

GARNISHES FOR SOUPS

One of the simplest garnishes for soup is a tablespoon of salted whipped cream sprinkled with a dash of paprika or a little very finely chopped parsley.

Eggs are used as garnishes of soups in the form of a baked custard cut in fancy shapes, or as egg balls. The whole yolks poached in salted water just below the boiling-point may be used; one yolk is served with each plate of soup.

Noodles, tapioca, spaghetti or macaroni cut in fancy shapes make simple and attractive garnishes for soup.

Cooked vegetables cut in thin strips or in Julienne style or in fancy shapes or slices, are often used to add color, flavor and nutritive value to a soup. Soups may also be garnished with cubes of bread or puff paste buttered and browned in the oven or fried in deep fat.

GARNISHES FOR EGG DISHES

Eggs are usually served with toast in some form. They may be garnished with crisp slices of bacon and a spray of parsley or they may be served on a bed of chopped spinach, mashed potato or chopped meat. A sauce or purée is a very attractive garnish for poached eggs. Eggs are sometimes garnished with grated cheese or cooked egg-yolk put through a sieve.

GARNISHES FOR VEGETABLES

Mashed vegetables are sometimes garnished with bits of butter and a sprinkling of paprika or finely chopped parsley. Vegetables that are cooked and served whole are often covered with grated cheese and put in the oven long enough to brown the cheese. Slices of hard-cooked eggs or egg-yolk put through a sieve may be used as a garnish for spinach.

GARNISHES FOR MEAT, FISH, GAME AND POULTRY

Roasts of beef, lamb or mutton may be garnished with browned potatoes, croquettes of rice or potatoes, mashed potato cups filled with green peas or diced vegetables, or slices of carrot, parsnip or turnip sautéd or fried in deep fat or with boiled onions and sprays of parsley or cress.

Roast pork may be garnished with any of the above or with baked apple or sautéd apple rings filled with jelly.

Fried bananas make a suitable garnish for roast of mutton.

Chops and steaks may be served with a simple garnish of parsley or cress and a slice of lemon or in a border of French fried potatoes, Saratoga chips or lattice potatoes.

Creamed meat dishes may be served with triangles or rounds of toast, in borders of rice or mashed potato, in croustades of bread, in timbale cases or patty shells or in cups of rice or mashed potato.

Sausage, meat balls or chops are attractively arranged about a mound of rice, mashed potato, macaroni or spinach.

Roast or fried chicken may be served in a border of celery or of fried oysters or with a simple garnish of parsley or cress.

Roast duck is attractive with endive and slices of orange and olives or with rice cups filled with currant jelly; roast goose with broiled sausage, gooseberry sauce, apple or barberry jelly or cooked rings of apple; roast quail with squares of fried mush and cubes of currant jelly.

Fish steaks, broiled fish or baked fish are usually garnished with slices of lemon and parsley or cress. Slices of hard-cooked eggs are often used as a garnish for fish. Fat fish such as salmon may be garnished with slices of cucumber or of tomato or whole tomatoes stuffed. Fish may also be garnished with potatoes, peas, onions or tomato in any form.

Other garnishes that may be used to give color are olives, radishes, mushroom caps, small green pickles, strips of green pepper or pimiento.

GARNISHES FOR SALADS AND DESSERTS

The best and simplest frame for any salad is a bed of lettuce leaves or shredded lettuce, cabbage or cress. Many salads are made more attractive by a sprinkling of chopped nuts or capers, minced green pepper or red pimiento or a grating of cheese. A half of a nut-meat, two or three radishes cut to resemble roses, dates or prunes stuffed with nuts or cream cheese, olives whole or sliced, tiny new onions or sliced green pickles all add flavor and color.

One of the most attractive garnishes for desserts is sweetened whipped cream either plain, sprinkled with chopped nuts, cinnamon or preserved ginger or topped with a candied or maraschino cherry or a bit of jam or preserve for color. A substitute for whipped cream may be made from the whites of two eggs beaten stiff with the mashed pulp of one banana slowly added, seasoned with lemon-juice and sugar to taste.

Meringues also serve to garnish such desserts as pastries and puddings.

TRUFFLES

Truffles are tuberous underground vegetables that are raised principally in France. They are too expensive to be used in large quantity but are highly prized as a flavorful garnish for aspics, salads and sauces. Because of their black color they make an effective contrast to the pale or vivid colors of the more common foods.

BUTTERED CRUMBS

Melt one to three tablespoons of butter, but do not brown it. Add one cup bread-crumbs, and mix with a fork until all the crumbs are covered.

BROWNED BREAD-CRUMBS

Brown the melted fat, being careful not to scorch it. Add the crumbs and brown slowly, stirring constantly. Serve hot.

This is a convenient way to prepare crumbs when an oven is not available.

FISH

BAKED HALIBUT STEAK

2 pounds halibut steak
Butter or other fat

1 cup milk
Pepper and salt

Rub steaks well with butter or other fat, pepper and salt. Lay steaks in baking-pan and pour the milk over them. Baste often while cooking, until all the milk is used. Serve with mushroom sauce.

HALIBUT CREOLE (BAKED)

2 pounds halibut
2 cups stewed tomatoes
1 cup water
3 cloves
1 slice onion

2 tablespoons butter or other fat
1 tablespoon flour
Salt and pepper

Put the tomatoes, water, cloves and onion on the stove in a stew-pan to boil. Mix the butter or other fat and flour together, stir them into the sauce when it boils and add the salt and pepper. Cook ten minutes and strain into a bowl.

Pour boiling water into a deep plate to the depth of one-half inch, and lay the fish in it for one minute, skin side down; when the fish is removed from the water, the black skin can be taken off easily. Wash the fish in cold water, season with salt and pepper and lay it on the baking sheet in a dripping-pan, put sliced lemon on top, then pour half the tomato sauce around the fish and bake for thirty to forty-five minutes, basting three times with the remainder of the tomato sauce. Pour the sauce remaining in the bottom of the pan around the fish on the serving platter.

CREAM SCALLOPS

1 pint scallops, fresh or canned   1 pint thin white sauce

Wash and drain the scallops, add them to the sauce and cook about fifteen minutes in a double boiler.

FILLET OF FLOUNDER AU GRATIN

5 pounds flounder
2 tablespoons flour
3 tablespoons butter or other fat
1 cup fine bread-crumbs

1 bay-leaf
2 cups chicken stock
1 tablespoon lemon-juice
1 slice onion
Salt and pepper

Fillet and cut the fish into pieces about four inches long by three wide. Oil a baking or gratin dish and lay the fillets in it. Sprinkle salt and pepper over them and set in a cool place till needed.

Rub together flour and fat; add onion, bay-leaf, chicken stock, and salt and pepper as needed. Simmer gently twenty minutes and then add lemon-juice, strain the sauce and pour it over the fish. Season lightly with salt and pepper, sprinkle bread-crumbs over the sauce and fish. Bake twenty minutes in a hot oven and serve at once in the same dish.

SALMON PUFFS

2 cups cooked salmon, fresh or canned
Salt and pepper

½ cup soft bread-crumbs
1 tablespoon lemon-juice
3 eggs

Remove the skin and bones from the salmon, chop the meat fine, and add salt, white pepper or paprika, soft bread-crumbs, lemon-juice or vinegar, and well beaten eggs. Mix thoroughly, and pack in six or eight oiled cups, filling the cups even full. Set the cups at once in a pan containing hot water that comes to about an inch below their tops, and bake for one-half hour. If the oven is very hot, lay a sheet of thick paper over the cups. Turn out upon a hot platter, thrust a sprig of parsley or celery, or a clove, into the center of each puff, and pour about them any good fish sauce.

CODFISH À LA MODE

1 cup salt codfish
2 cups mashed potatoes
2 cups milk or cream

2 eggs
¼ cup butter or other fat
Pepper

Pick very fine and freshen salt codfish. Mix with mashed potatoes, milk or cream, well-beaten egg, butter or other fat and pepper. Bake in an earthen dish twenty or twenty-five minutes.

SCALLOPED CLAMS

18 opened clams	48 very small dice of fat bacon
6 large clams in shell	4 tablespoons cracker-dust
White pepper	2 tablespoons butter
2 tablespoons minced celery	

Have the clams that are in the shell opened carefully, so as not to injure the shells, which are to be used in scalloping the clams. Clean the shells well with brush and water. Lay two clams in each half shell, dust with white pepper, and one-half teaspoon of minced celery, and add four of the bacon dice; cover with a very thin layer of cracker-dust, put a half teaspoon butter on top and bake in the oven until brown.

CREAMED LOBSTER

1 cup milk	½ teaspoon pepper
1 cup cream or evaporated milk	¼ teaspoon paprika

Make a white sauce with the fat, flour and milk. Add lobster cut into small pieces and salt and pepper. Some cooks add a teaspoon of curry-powder.

Sometimes this preparation is placed in greased or oiled scallop shells, sprinkled with fine seasoned bread or cracker-crums and browned in the oven.

SHRIMPS IN PEPPERS

2 cups cooked shrimps, fresh or canned	Nutmeg
	Celery seed
1 tablespoon butter	1 egg
½ teaspoon mustard	½ cup bread-crums
Pepper	6 green peppers

Prepare shrimps as directed. Cut off the stem ends or tops of the peppers, and remove the seeds and veins, and soak the peppers in cold water for one-half hour. Cream the butter by heating and then also beat into it the seasonings and egg. Add the crums, mixing the ingredients well, and finally stirring in the shrimps. Drain the peppers and fill with the prepared stuffing. Set them in a pan, open side up, and bake in a hot oven for twenty minutes.

LITTLE PIGS IN BLANKETS

24 large oysters
24 very thin short slices fat bacon

Salt and pepper
Parsley

Season the oysters with salt and pepper. Wrap one oyster in each slice of bacon and fasten with a toothpick. Heat a saucepan and put in the little pigs; cook just long enough to crisp the bacon, about five minutes. Cut slices of toast into quarters and place one pig in its blanket on each small slice of toast. Serve immediately, garnished with parsley.

BAKED OYSTERS

30 oysters in the shell
Butter

Salt and pepper

Wash the oyster shells thoroughly by scrubbing with a brush. Place with the deep shell down in a baking-pan in a very hot oven, bake until the shells open, remove the upper shells, add a little butter, salt and pepper to each oyster, and serve in the undershells.

FISH THAT ARE GOOD BOILED

With Suggestions for Sauces and Garnishes

Fish	Sauce	Garnish
Codfish	Butter sauce, caper sauce, oyster sauce, shrimp sauce	Parsley or cress
Flounder	Béchamel sauce	Chopped parsley
Haddock	Egg sauce	Parsley or cress
Halibut	Béchamel sauce, creamy sauce, egg sauce, Hollandaise sauce	Parsley or cress
Mackerel	Caper sauce, parsley sauce	
Salmon	Egg sauce, Hollandaise sauce, Tartar sauce	Cress, lemon, parsley
Snapper (red)	Mushroom sauce, tomato sauce	Parsley
Sole (flounder)	Béchamel sauce	Parsley
Trout	Horseradish sauce	

FISH THAT MAY BE BROILED

With Suggestions for Sauces and Garnishes

Fish	Sauce	Garnish
Cod	Melted butter	Lemon
Flounder	Tomato sauce, lemon sauce	Parsley
Halibut	Butter sauce, Hollandaise sauce, oyster sauce	Parsley, lemon
Mackerel	Maître d'hôtel sauce, lemon sauce	Lemon, cucumber, parsley
Salmon	Anchovy sauce, caper sauce	Chopped parsley
Shad	Maître d'hôtel sauce, butter sauce	Parsley and radishes
Smelts	Rémoulade sauce, Béchamel sauce	

FISH THAT MAY BE BAKED WHOLE

With Suggestions for Stuffings, Sauces and Garnishes

Fish	Stuffing	Sauce	Garnish
Bass (sea)	Bread stuffing	Tomato sauce	Tomato and parsley
Bluefish	Bread stuffing	Tomato sauce	Parsley and lemon slices
Cod	Oyster stuffing	Oyster sauce	Lemon
Haddock	Pickle-caper	Drawn butter, egg sauce, Hollandaise sauce	Lemon and parsley
Mackerel	Pickle-caper		Lemon
Shad	Bread stuffing		Lemon, tomatoes
Whitefish	Bread stuffing	Egg sauce	Egg
	Pickle-caper	Hollandaise sauce	Lemon

MEAT

BRISKET WITH ONION SAUCE

3 pounds beef brisket
Soup greens
Cloves
Peppercorns
Salt
1 egg

Crums
½ cup green onions
2 tablespoons fat
2 tablespoons flour
1½ cups stock
1 tablespoon minced parsley

Wipe the meat with a damp cloth, and tie it into a compact shape with strips of cloth. Place it in a deep kettle with boiling water (or part of the stock, if possible). Add a bunch of soup greens, several cloves and peppercorns. Simmer until the meat is tender, add salt when partly cooked. Take the meat from the liquid, remove the cloth, and place meat in a shallow baking-dish. Beat one egg and spread over the beef, then sprinkle with coarse crums and brown under a flame or in a hot oven. Serve with onion sauce made as follows: Cut up the onions and brown them in the fat. Make a brown sauce of the fat, flour and stock. Add the parsley and serve.

OLD-FASHIONED BOILED DINNER

6 pounds corned-beef brisket
1 cabbage
3 white turnips

4 carrots
6 potatoes
6 beets
Vinegar

Put the meat into the pot over a brisk fire with enough cold water to cover it. Bring it rapidly just to the boiling-point, then remove the scum, set the pot back on the fire and simmer until tender (about three hours). About three-fourths of an hour before serving, skim the liquid free from fat. Put a portion of this liquor into another kettle with the cabbage which has been cleaned and cut into sections, the turnips, carrots and parsnips prepared and cut into uniform pieces, and boil until tender.

46

SAVORY BEEF

2 pounds beef, plate, shank, rump or round
3 large onions, sliced
3 tablespoons fat
3 tablespoons flour
1 teaspoon salt
¼ teaspoon black pepper
¼ teaspoon ground cloves and thyme or Summer savory
1 pint brown stock or boiling water and meat extract
2 tablespoons vinegar
1 tablespoon catchup

Brown the onions slowly in fat. Increase the heat. Cut meat into sizes desired for serving, add it to the onions, and brown. Mix the flour, pepper and other seasonings. Sprinkle this mixture over the meat. Add the stock, vinegar and catchup. Cover closely. Simmer until meat is tender, allowing at least two hours for shank or plate and one and one-half hour for rump or round.

POT ROAST

3 to 4 pounds chuck, round, rump or brisket
Flour
3 tablespoons fat, preferably from salt pork
1 cup sliced carrots
1 cup sliced onions
1 cup chopped celery
1 cup sliced turnips

If the meat is not in a solid piece, skewer or tie it into shape, wipe it with a damp cloth and roll it in flour. Heat the fat in a frying-pan or Dutch oven. Put in the meat and brown on all sides. If the frying-pan is used, transfer the meat, after it is brown, to a kettle deep enough to hold the beef and vegetables when the cover is on. Cover tightly and let simmer slowly for from four to five hours, turning twice. Add the vegetables at the end of four hours' cooking. After removing the meat and vegetables, thicken the gravy by adding one to two tablespoons of flour mixed with cold water for each cup of broth.

BEEFSTEAK PIE

2 pounds rump, flank or chuck steak
Pie paste
Chopped onion
Salt and pepper
Sliced potatoes
Butter
Flour
Egg

Cut the meat into strips two inches long by one inch wide. Put them with the bone, just cover them with water and simmer until partly done. Line a baking-dish with pie paste, put in a layer of meat with a little finely sliced onion, salt and pepper, next a layer of sliced potatoes, with a bit of butter on each slice. Alternate the steak and potato layers until the dish is full. Thicken the gravy with browned flour and pour in, put on a top crust, brush it with beaten egg and bake until quite brown.

BEEFSTEAK WITH OYSTERS

1 steak	1 tablespoon sifted flour
1 quart oysters	3 tablespoons butter

Set the oysters, with a very little of their juice, over the fire; when they come to a boil, remove any scum and stir in the butter, in which the sifted flour has been rubbed. Boil one minute, pour over the steak and serve at once.

PLANKED STEAK

1 steak 2 inches thick	Butter
Duchess potatoes	Chopped parsley
Various kinds of cooked vege-	Salt
tables	Paprika

Trim the fat and make outline of the steak even. Sear it on both sides on a hot griddle or pan, using no fat. Cook fifteen minutes, turning frequently. Oil a heated plank, place the steak on the plank, and arrange border of Duchess potatoes around it. Arrange other cooked vegetables, such as stuffed tomatoes or green peppers, small boiled onions, peas, string beans and cubes of carrot or turnip, around the steak, also, so that the board is entirely concealed. Place the plank in the oven until the potato border is browned and all the vegetables are heated through. After removing it from the oven, spread the steak with butter into which has been rubbed finely chopped parsley, salt and paprika. Send to table upon the plank.

BAKED HAMBURG STEAK

1½ pounds beef round
2 cups bread soaked in milk
1 small onion
1 tablespoon butter
2 eggs

4 hard-cooked eggs
1 cup tomatoes
½ cup sliced onion
Salt, pepper, ginger

Chop the meat fine. Add the bread, one minced onion, seasonings to taste and the two uncooked eggs, well beaten. Arrange the hard-cooked eggs end to end across the middle of the meat and roll the meat mixture around them. Place the roll in a baking-pan, pour over it a sauce composed of the tomatoes, sliced onions, butter and water, and bake, basting frequently with sauce. In serving, slice the roll crosswise. The hard-cooked eggs may be omitted.

BEEF LOAF

1½ pounds round steak
2 eggs
1½ cups bread-crums

2 tablespoons chopped parsley
½ teaspoon pepper
2 teaspoons salt

Chop the steak. Mix it thoroughly with the unbeaten eggs, bread-crums, chopped parsley, pepper and salt. Place in a bread-pan and press firmly until it is molded to the shape of the pan. Run a sharp thin knife-blade around the loaf, turn it out into a roasting-pan, place in a moderate oven and bake for about two hours, basting every quarter of an hour with hot stock. Cut in thin slices, and serve cold with horseradish. A hard-cooked egg may be molded in the center of the loaf to show prettily when sliced.

SCALLOPED CORNED BEEF

2 cups cooked corned beef cut
  into cubes
1 cup medium white sauce
Butter

1 stalk celery
2 slices onion
Bread-crums

Cook chopped celery and onions in the sauce. Put the corned-beef in a shallow baking-dish and add the sauce. Sprinkle with bread-crums moistened with melted butter. Brown in a hot oven.

CORNED-BEEF HASH

2 cups chopped corned beef
2 cups cooked potatoes
Salt and pepper

½ cup milk or water
2 tablespoons butter, or savory
    fat

Mix beef and potatoes together lightly and season. Pour the milk into a frying-pan with half the fat and, when this is warm, turn in the hash, spreading it evenly and placing the rest of the fat, cut in pieces, on the top. Cover the pan and place it where the hash will cook slowly for half an hour. There should then be a rich, thick crust on the bottom. Do not stir the hash. Fold it as an omelet is folded and place it on a warm platter. This slow process of heating the hash gives it a flavor that can not be obtained by hurried cooking.

VEAL CUTLETS WITH CREAM GRAVY

2 pounds veal cutlets
Salt and pepper
Egg
Bread or cracker-crumbs

Drippings
1 cup milk or cream
1 tablespoon flour

Wipe the cutlets, sprinkle with salt and pepper, dip them first in beaten egg and then in fine bread or cracker-crumbs, and sauté in drippings until brown. If preferred, they may be cut into small pieces of similar size and pounded with a rolling-pin until little more than a quarter of an inch in thickness and then egged and crumbed and sautéd. The cutlets should be thoroughly browned on both sides. Place them on a platter, add cream to the gravy in the pan, and thicken slightly with flour rubbed to a smooth paste with a little cold water. They may be served with slices of bacon. Tomato sauce may be used instead of milk sauce.

VEAL COLLOPS

2 pounds veal
Egg

Cracker-crums
Salt and pepper

Cut the veal in pieces the size of an oyster, dip in beaten egg, roll in cracker-crums and season with salt and pepper. Fry in deep fat.

STUFFED BREAST OF VEAL

4 pounds breast of veal	**1** teaspoon sweet marjoram
1 cup bread-crumbs	**1** teaspoon thyme
2 slices fat salt pork	**1** teaspoon salt
¼ teaspoon pepper	

The butcher will prepare the veal for stuffing, if requested to do so. If he has not done so, make an incision between the ribs and the meat, to form a cavity. Fill this cavity with stuffing made from the bread-crums, pork, sweet marjoram, thyme, salt and pepper. Roast, following directions for roast veal.

MUTTON STEW

2 pounds neck, plate or shoulder of mutton	6 onions
	Salt and pepper
2 pounds potatoes	3 to 4 cups hot water

Cut the mutton into small pieces and arrange in a stew-pan. Sprinkle with salt and pepper, and add the hot water. Cover closely and let the stew simmer for one hour, shaking the pan occasionally. Add the potatoes and onions, peeled and sliced, and cook another hour. Serve very hot. If desired, dumplings may be served with this stew.

ROAST LEG OF MUTTON

1 leg of mutton	Salt and pepper
Flour	

Wipe the mutton with a damp cloth, remove the outside skin and excess of fat, sprinkle it with salt, pepper and flour, and place on a rack in a roasting-pan. Allow fifteen or twenty minutes to a pound for roasting. When the meat is done, remove it from the pan. Also remove all except one tablespoon of the fat. In this, brown two tablespoons flour, add one and one-half cups boiling water, and stir constantly until it thickens. Cook two minutes. Season to taste and strain. Serve as gravy.

ROAST SPARERIBS

Pork spareribs	Powdered sage (may be omitted)
Salt and pepper	
Flour	Minced onion
Bread-crumbs	Butter, fat or cooking oil

Trim the ends of the ribs neatly, crack them across the middle, and sprinkle with salt and pepper. Cover the meat with greased paper and leave this paper on until the meat is half done; then remove the paper and dredge the meat with flour. In ten minutes, baste with butter, fat or cooking oil, and afterward baste every fifteen minutes with the gravy. This is a necessity, as this meat is very dry. Just before taking the pork from the oven, strew its surface with bread-crums mixed with the seasonings. Cook five minutes, and baste once more. Make the gravy as directed for roast leg of pork, strain, and pour it over the meat, or serve in a gravy-dish.

CROWN ROAST OF PORK

1 crown of pork
Cubes of salt pork
Mashed potatoes
Steamed apples
Salt and pepper
Cranberries

Select ribs of a young pig and have the butcher make a crown, like a crown roast of lamb or mutton. Cover the tip of each bone with salt pork. Roast as spareribs are roasted, and serve with mashed potatoes inside the crown and a border of bright red steamed apples as a garnish. The apples should be of uniform size and steamed, rather than baked, to preserve their color. Remove the cubes of salt pork and cap each bone with a large cranberry, or with a paper frill.

FRESH PORK WITH VEGETABLES

1 pound pork butt
4 large carrots
4 large parsnips
1 small red cabbage
Seasoning

Boil the piece of pork one and one-half hours. Cook the vegetables in the same kettle until they are soft, then remove them and finish cooking the meat. Cut the pork into thin slices. Arrange them side by side down the middle of a large platter, and make a border of the cabbage, quartered, and the other vegetables cut into lengths.

BAKED HAM

1 ham
Brown sugar
Soft bread-crums
1 teaspoon mustard
Whole cloves

Boil the ham whole, and skin it. Cut off some of the superfluous fat. Mix brown sugar and soft bread-crums, in the proportion of four parts sugar to one of crums, add one teaspoon mustard, and spread the mixture over the ham. Insert cloves about one inch apart, making a diamond pattern. Bake one-half hour, or until well glazed.

PREPARING SWEETBREADS

Sweetbreads should be plunged into cold water as soon as they are received, and soaked for one hour, then they should be par-boiled in acidulated, salted water (one teaspoon salt and one tablespoon vinegar to one quart water) for twenty minutes. After draining they should be plunged into cold water again to make them firm. The little strings and membranes, which are easily detached after parboiling, should be removed.

FRIED SWEETBREADS

2 pairs sweetbreads	Salt and pepper
2 tablespoons flour	Egg
1 cup milk	Bread or cracker-crums

Prepare as directed and cut in even-sized slices. Sprinkle with salt and pepper, dip in beaten egg and crums and fry in deep fat. When well browned on both sides, place them on a platter. Make a sauce with two tablespoons of the fat in which the sweet-breads were fried, the flour and milk and season with salt and pepper.

Fried sweetbreads are often served with green peas, placed in a mound or a little hill in the center of the platter. Macaroni may be boiled very tender and laid on the platter and the sweet-breads placed in the center, the pipes of the macaroni being laid about them in the form of a nest.

CREAMED SWEETBREADS

2 pairs sweetbreads	2 cups milk
4 tablespoons butter or other fat	1 cup cream or evaporated milk
4 tablespoons flour	¼ teaspoon paprika

Prepare as directed and cut into dice. Make a white sauce with the fat, flour and milk or cream, add the sweetbreads, and stir steadily until very hot. Season with salt and pepper and minced parsley.

VIRGINIA BEEF TONGUE

1 beef tongue, fresh	¼ cup butter or fat
1 cup brown sugar	1 tablespoon whole cloves
1 cup stewed cranberries	½ lemon

Scrub the tongue and simmer it until tender, in water to cover. Remove the skin and trim the root end. Take one cup of the liquor in which the tongue was cooked and add the brown sugar, stewed cranberries, butter or other fat, cloves, and lemon, sliced. Simmer the tongue in this mixture for one-fourth hour. Place on a dish with the sauce, garnish with slices of lemon and sprigs of parsley, and serve.

Tongue may be jellied and served cold.

BROILED KIDNEYS

6 lamb's or 4 calf's kidneys	Butter
Cooking oil	Lemon
Salt and pepper	Parsley

Cut the kidneys into halves, remove the white tubes and fat and cover with cold water for thirty minutes. Drain and dry on a piece of cheese-cloth. Brush with, or dip into, cooking oil. Broil slowly until brown on both sides. Remove from the broiler and put in pan, sprinkle with salt, pepper and a little melted butter. Cover the pan and set over a slow fire for a few minutes. Serve garnished with slices of lemon and sprigs of parsley.

USING LEFT-OVERS OF MEAT

Almost any left-over meat or fish may be made into a palatable dish. In general, these are the rules to follow:

1. Trim off carefully all non-edible parts.

2. Cut or shape meat in pieces of uniform size. Do not wash.

3. Since the meat is already cooked, it should be protected from direct heat by sauce, crums, potatoes or the cereal which is used with it.

4. Sauces should be thoroughly cooked before adding meat to them.

5. Season left-over meat dishes rather highly. Sweet herbs, onions, celery salt, paprika, curry or tabasco may be used.

6. In general, when a sauce or gravy is used, take half as much sauce as the measure of meat and vegetable.

POULTRY AND GAME

ROAST CHICKEN

1 roasting chicken
Stuffing
Savory fat or olive oil

Salt and pepper
Flour

Wash, singe and draw the fowl, rub it with salt and pepper inside and out, and stuff the fowl. (Any stuffing may be used. Bread stuffing, chestnut stuffing and celery stuffing are particularly good.) Truss and tie the fowl. Grease it well with savory fat or olive oil, dredge with flour and place it on a trivet in a double roasting-pan in a hot oven (480° Fahrenheit), to sear quickly so that its juices may not escape during the roasting. After twenty or twenty-five minutes, when the skin is well seared, cover the pan, lessen the heat to 370° and cook until the breast is tender. If cooked in an open pan, as soon as the flour has been nicely browned, baste well, adding a little fat or water if necessary, repeating the basting every ten minutes. Allow about twenty minutes to a pound for roasting. Serve with giblet sauce.

CHICKEN, MARYLAND STYLE

1 chicken
2 tablespoons flour
Salt and pepper

1 cup milk or cream
½ cup butter or other fat

Clean and disjoint chicken, leaving the breast whole. Put the neck and giblets into cold water and cook so as to obtain a cup of stock for the gravy. Arrange the chicken in a pan, being careful that no piece touches another. Sprinkle with salt and pepper, dredge with flour, and dot over with half of the butter or other fat. Bake in a hot oven from thirty to forty minutes, basting frequently with one-fourth cup of butter melted in one-fourth cup of hot water.

When the chicken is done, make a gravy from the fat left in the pan, stirring in two tablespoons of flour, one cup of milk or cream and the cup of stock made from the giblets. If desired, add a few button mushrooms. Serve the chicken with the gravy poured around it.

SMOTHERED CHICKEN

2 small chickens or 1 large one
Salt and pepper
Flour

2 or more tablespoons butter
or other fat

This is one of the most delicious ways of cooking chicken. Take off the neck and split the chicken down the back, wiping it with a damp towel. Season inside and out with salt and pepper, and dredge on all sides with flour. Lay the chicken, with the inside down, in a small baking-tin, and add a very little water. The pan should be very little larger than the chickens, otherwise the gravy will be too quickly evaporated. Cook slowly for one hour, basting every ten minutes after the first twenty minutes, or cook in a covered baking-pan.

Should the chicken be decidedly lacking in fat, add butter or other fat. There will be plenty of gravy in the pan with which to baste if the pan is small. When done, place the chicken on a hot platter, add enough water to make two cups gravy and thicken with two tablespoons flour. Should the chicken be quite fat, remove all but two tablespoons of the oil from the pan before making the gravy. Season with salt and pepper, pour it over the chicken and serve at once.

CHICKEN POT-PIE

1 chicken
3 tablespoons flour
Salt and pepper

1 teaspoon salt
1 cup milk

Clean, singe and cut up the chicken, place it in a pot and nearly cover with water. Cover the pot and simmer gently. An old fowl will require at least three or four hours' slow cooking, but a year-old chicken should be done in one and one-half hours. Remove the cover during the last half-hour of cooking, to reduce the gravy to about one and one-half pints when done.

Three-fourths of an hour before time to serve, make dumplings, add to the chicken and cover. When the dumplings are done and ready to serve, add salt and pepper to the chicken and make the gravy by adding to the liquor in the kettle three tablespoons of flour stirred to a paste in one cup of milk. Skim out the chicken, lay it on a platter, place the dumplings on the top and pour over them the gravy.

FRICASSEED CHICKEN

1 chicken
2 tablespoons butter or other fat
2 cups chicken stock
2 tablespoons flour
1 cup milk or cream

1 egg-yolk
Salt and pepper
Herbs
Salt pork
Rice or dumplings

Singe, clean and cut up the chicken. Brown in a pan with the butter, drippings or chicken fat. Cover with boiling water, add salt, pepper, herbs and a few slices of salt pork. Simmer until tender (about an hour), strain and thicken one pint of the liquor with the flour mixed to a smooth paste with a little cold water; add the milk or cream beaten with the yolk of the egg. Heat again until slightly thickened, pour over the chicken and serve with rice or dumplings.

ROAST TURKEY

Follow directions for roast chicken. An eight-pound turkey should be allowed three hours in a moderate oven (350-480° F.). It may be dredged with flour a second time about one hour before it is to be served. Serve with giblet sauce.

ROAST GOOSE WITH POTATO STUFFING

1 goose (about 8 pounds)
Potato stuffing
Salt pork if goose is not fat

Salt and pepper
Flour

Select a goose that is about four months old; an old goose is better braized than roasted. Singe the goose, wash it carefully in hot water, and wipe it dry before drawing it. Flatten the breast-bone by striking it with a rolling-pin. Partly fill the goose with potato stuffing, stitch up the openings and truss it. If it is not fat, lay thin slices of pork upon the breast, but if the goose has considerable fat, omit the pork. Bake in a hot oven (400-480° F.) for forty-five minutes, remove it from the oven, pour out all the fat, sprinkle the bird all over with salt and pepper, dredge with flour, and return it to the oven.

When the flour is a good brown, pour one cup of hot water into the pan and baste the goose often, dredging it each time with a slight sifting of flour to absorb the fat. Allow eighteen minutes to the pound for a young goose and twenty-five for one that is old. Remove the goose from the pan, add a cup of hot water to the gravy and thicken it, if necessary, with browned flour. Garnish the goose with parsley and serve with giblet gravy.

Apple sauce is often served with roast goose.

Goslings may be roasted in the same way, allowing, however, only fifteen minutes to the pound for cooking.

ROAST GOOSE WITH BAKED APPLE

1 eight-pound goose	1/4 teaspoon sage
2 cups bread-crums	1 teaspoon salt
1 chopped onion	Pinch of pepper
2 tablespoons fat	6 to 8 apples
3 sweet potatoes	1/4 cup brown sugar

Cook the giblets until tender, chop and add to stuffing made by mixing bread-crums, onion, fat, sage, salt and pepper. After cleaning and washing the goose thoroughly, stuff, and sew the neck and back. Roast very slowly (350-400° F.), about three hours. Wash and core six to eight apples; sprinkle with sugar, stuff with mashed and seasoned sweet potato. Bake until tender and serve hot with the goose.

ROAST DUCK

Epicures prefer young ducks, cooked rare, and when so prepared they are not stuffed. Should filling be preferred, use potato stuffing, putting it in very hot. Some people consider that ducks have a strong flavor, and to absorb this flavor lay cored and quartered apples inside the body. These apples are removed before the duck is sent to the table. Celery and onions also may be placed inside the duck to season it and improve the flavor, two tablespoons of chopped onion being used to every cup of chopped celery, which may consist of the green stalks that are not desired for the table. This stuffing is also removed from the bird before it is sent to the table.

Truss the duck, sprinkle it with salt, pepper and flour, and roast in a very hot oven (400-480° F.) fifteen to thirty minutes, provided the duck is young and is desired rare. Full-grown domestic ducks should be roasted at least one hour in an oven only moderately hot and should be basted every ten minutes. Serve with giblet gravy and apple sauce or grape or currant jelly. Green peas should also be served with roast duck.

STUFFINGS FOR FISH, MEAT, POULTRY AND GAME

BREAD STUFFING—No. 1

1½ cups bread-crums
1 teaspoon salt
¼ teaspoon pepper

½ cup milk
1 tablespoon chopped onion
1 tablespoon butter

Add the seasonings and butter to the crums and beat in the milk last.

BREAD STUFFING—No. 2

1½ cups bread-crums
3 tablespoons butter or other fat
1 tablespoon chopped onion

1 teaspoon powdered sage
1 teaspoon salt
¼ teaspoon pepper

Rub the fat into the crums, then add the seasonings.

POTATO STUFFING

2 cups hot mashed potato
1 cup bread-crums
½ teaspoon pepper
½ tablespoon salt

1 teaspoon sage
4 tablespoons melted butter or other fat
2 tablespoons onion-juice

Mix the ingredients in the order given.

CELERY STUFFING

½ bunch celery
2 tablespoons butter or other fat
2 eggs

1 quart stale but not dry bread-crums
2 tablespoons salt
½ teaspoon pepper

Chop the celery fine. Melt the butter or other fat, add the crums and mix well. Add the celery, salt and pepper and the eggs slightly beaten.

OYSTER STUFFING

1 pint oysters
1 teaspoon salt
¼ teaspoon pepper

2 cups dry bread-crums
¼ cup butter or other fat

Mix the oysters well with the bread-crums and seasoning, and add melted butter or other fat.

SAUSAGE STUFFING

½ pound sausage-meat
2 cups dried bread-crums
Salt and pepper

1 tablespoon onion-juice
1 tablespoon minced parsley

Mix sausage and crums, then add seasonings.

MUSHROOM STUFFING

3 cups stale bread-crums
6 tablespoons butter or other fat
½ cup chopped mushrooms

2 teaspoons salt
½ teaspoon powdered thyme
1 teaspoon minced parsley

Mix ingredients in the order given.

CHESTNUT STUFFING

1 quart chestnuts
¼ cup bread-crums
2 tablespoons butter or other fat

2 tablespoons cream
Salt and pepper
Onion-juice, if desired

Shell and blanch the chestnuts and cook in boiling water until tender. While they are still hot, rub them through a coarse sieve or colander. Add other ingredients in order given.

SAUCES FOR FISH, MEAT, POULTRY AND GAME

WHITE SAUCE AND BROWN SAUCE

Equal parts of fat and flour make the best roux for thickening sauces. If much more fat than flour is used, the fat rises to the top of the mixture; if less flour than fat is used, the paste may burn. Therefore, if less fat than flour is required, it is better not to make it into a roux but to use another method of thickening the sauce. If more fat than flour is required in the sauce, it should be beaten in in small pieces after the liquid is added and just before the sauce is served.

The American method of making roux is to melt the butter, add the flour and cook only until the mixture bubbles before adding the liquid. This saves time, but at the expense of the flavor of the sauce. The French method is to melt the fat, add the flour and cook with constant stirring for five minutes, to remove the raw taste of the flour.

For a brown roux, the basis of brown sauces, the butter is melted and allowed to brown before the flour is added. After the addition of the flour, it is allowed to cook until the flour, too, is brown. This long cooking is the secret of a successful brown sauce.

All sauces thickened with flour or corn-starch should be cooked for at least fifteen minutes; an hour or longer improves the flavor. The seasonings should be added just before the sauce is served.

THIN WHITE SAUCE

1 tablespoon flour	$\frac{1}{4}$ teaspoon salt
1 teaspoon to 1 tablespoon fat	$\frac{1}{8}$ teaspoon pepper
1 cup milk	

MEDIUM WHITE SAUCE

2 to 3 tablespoons flour	$\frac{1}{4}$ teaspoon salt
1 to 3 tablespoons fat	$\frac{1}{8}$ teaspoon pepper
1 cup milk	

THICK WHITE SAUCE

4 to 5 tablespoons flour   ¼ teaspoon salt
1 to 5 tablespoons fat   ⅛ teaspoon pepper
1 cup milk

VELOUTÉ SAUCE

Substitute one cup of well-seasoned white stock for the milk in thin or medium white sauce.

POULETTE SAUCE

1 cup Velouté sauce   1 cup cream
2 egg-yolks

Slowly add, with constant stirring, the Velouté to the egg-yolks, beat in the cream and reheat over hot water. Beat well and serve at once. It is improved by adding a little at a time, one tablespoon butter, the juice of half a lemon, a tablespoon of chopped parsley and a dash of nutmeg.

PERSILLADE SAUCE (PARSLEY SAUCE)

2 to 4 tablespoons chopped   1 cup medium or thin white
  parsley   sauce

Add parsley to white sauce.

CELERY SAUCE

½ cup chopped cooked celery   1 cup medium white sauce

Add celery to white sauce. Serve with boiled fowls.

CHEESE SAUCE

2 to 4 ounces cheese   1 cup medium or thin white
Mustard and paprika   sauce

Put the cheese through a food-chopper. Mix with the white sauce. Set over hot water and stir until the cheese is thoroughly blended with the sauce. Season with mustard and paprika.

EGG SAUCE

1 chopped hard-cooked egg   1 cup medium white sauce

Combine the two ingredients.

Broiled halibut steak garnished with lemon and orange slices and black grapes. This may be served with mushroom sauce.

Thin slices of bread, spread with cheese or fish paste, and then carefully rolled and toasted.

Cream cheese, whipped cream and gelatin combined to make a ring, served with tomato salad.

A platter of assorted fruits stuffed with cheese, to serve with the salad course.

OYSTER SAUCE

1 pint small oysters	1 cup medium white sauce seasoned

Heat the oysters in their own liquor to boiling-point. Remove them from the fire after they have boiled one-half minute, skim them, and combine with the white sauce.

TOMATO SAUCE

1 quart fresh or canned tomatoes	3 tablespoons butter
1 slice onion	3 tablespoons flour
8 cloves	Salt and pepper

Set the tomatoes, onion and cloves on the fire and cook for twenty minutes. Brown the fat in a frying-pan, add the flour, and cook until smooth and brown, stirring constantly. Add the tomatoes.

SAUCE PIQUANTE

2 tablespoons butter or other fat	2 cloves
2 onions	1 clove of garlic
2 carrots	2 tablespoons flour
2 shallots	1 cup beef or veal stock
Thyme	½ cup vinegar
1 bunch parsley	Salt and pepper

Melt butter or other fat, slice into it onions, carrots and shallots. Add a little thyme, minced parsley, cloves and clove of garlic. Let this mixture cook until the carrot is soft, then add flour. Let it cook for five minutes more, and add beef or veal stock and vinegar, skim, and strain through a sieve. Add salt and pepper when boiling.

HORSERADISH SAUCE

¼ cup heavy cream	¼ teaspoon salt
3 tablespoons grated horse-radish	Sprinkle cayenne or pepper
	1 tablespoon vinegar

Whip the cream until stiff. Gradually beat in mixture of other ingredients. Serve on baked ham.

GIBLET GRAVY

Giblets and neck of fowl   2 tablespoons flour
2 tablespoons chicken fat   Salt and pepper

Place the giblets (liver, heart and gizzard) and the neck in a
saucepan, and cover them with cold water. Simmer slowly and
when tender remove meat from the neck, and chop fine with the
giblets, saving the water in which they were cooked. Heat the
fat on top of the stove and when it is hot, stir in the flour. Cook
two minutes, then add one cup of the stock left from cooking the
giblets, pouring it in gradually so as not to thin the gravy too
much. If the gravy seems too thick, add a little hot water.
Lastly, put in the chopped giblets, and season to taste with salt
and pepper.

DRAWN-BUTTER SAUCE

⅓ cup butter   1 pint boiling water
4 tablespoons flour   ¼ teaspoon salt

Make a roux of four tablespoons of the butter and all of the
flour. Gradually add the boiling water, stirring constantly over
hot water, until the sauce comes to the boiling-point. Simmer
until it is thick and smooth. When ready to serve, add salt
and the remaining butter in small bits, beating constantly.

MAÎTRE D'HÔTEL SAUCE

2 cups drawn-butter sauce   2 egg-yolks
1 tablespoon lemon-juice   Salt and pepper
1 tablespoon chopped parsley

Add the lemon-juice and chopped parsley to the drawn-butter
sauce. Let it cool slightly, add the beaten yolks and season with
salt and pepper. Do not permit the sauce to boil after the addition of the egg-yolk.

CURRANT JELLY SAUCE

1 onion   1 stalk celery
1 tablespoon butter   1 bay-leaf
1 tablespoon flour   2 tablespoons vinegar
½ cup currant jelly   2 cups stock

Slice the onion and cook in the butter till it begins to color, then
add the flour and herbs and stir until brown. Add the vinegar

and the stock and simmer twenty minutes. Strain, skim off all the fat, put in the jelly and stir it until it is melted. This sauce is used with game.

MUSHROOM SAUCE

4 tablespoons butter or other fat

4 tablespoons flour

2 cups stock

1 cup mushrooms, fresh or canned

Salt and pepper

Make a brown sauce of the fat, flour and stock. Add one cup mushrooms and cook until hot. If mushrooms are not very gently treated, they will become tough. Too much cooking ruins them, three or four minutes being quite sufficient for those that have been canned and five or six for fresh ones.

This sauce is used with any kind of roasted, broiled or braized meat, particularly with beef.

OLIVE SAUCE

2 dozen olives

2 tablespoons salad oil

1 slice onion

1 lemon

2 tablespoons flour

1 pint stock

Salt and pepper

Place the olives in an earthenware bowl, cover with hot water and let them remain for half an hour to draw out the brine. Place the oil in a frying-pan, and add the onion; when this commences to color, add the flour. Stir until smooth. After it has cooked for two minutes, add the stock, and place where it will simmer gently. Pare the olives round and round as though paring an apple, leaving the pulp in a single strip. If this is done carefully, the olives will retain their shape. Place the olives in the sauce, add the seasoning, the juice of the lemon and simmer for twenty minutes. Skim carefully and serve.

HOLLANDAISE SAUCE

$\frac{1}{2}$ cup butter

Yolks of 3 eggs

Juice of $\frac{1}{2}$ lemon

1 teaspoon salt

$\frac{1}{4}$ teaspoon pepper

$\frac{1}{2}$ cup boiling water

This is one of the best sauces for fish. Beat the butter to a cream with a silver spoon, add the yolks of the eggs, one at a time, and beat well, then add the lemon-juice, salt and pepper.

About five minutes before serving, add the boiling water, a little at a time, stirring well. Place the bowl in a saucepan of boiling water, and stir rapidly until the sauce thickens like boiled custard.

TARTAR SAUCE

1 cup mayonnaise dressing
1 teaspoon onion-juice
1 tablespoon capers

1 tablespoon chopped cucumber pickle

Make the mayonnaise rather more sour and with a little more mustard than for salad, and mix into it the capers, pickle and onion-juice. Set on the ice until needed. This sauce should be quite thick when served.

MINT SAUCE

1 tablespoon powdered sugar
½ cup vinegar

¼ cup finely chopped mint leaves

Dissolve sugar in vinegar. Pour this over finely chopped mint leaves and stand for one-half hour on back of a stove to infuse. If vinegar is very strong, dilute with water.

PARSLEY BUTTER

3 tablespoons butter
1 tablespoon lemon-juice
1 tablespoon chopped parsley

½ teaspoon salt
⅛ teaspoon pepper

Cream butter and then add lemon-juice, chopped parsley, salt and pepper. This may be used to spread on fried or boiled fish or over potato balls. When intended for the latter, one-half tablespoon of lemon-juice will be enough.

JELLY SAUCE

1 glass currant or grape jelly
1 level teaspoon dry mustard

1 teaspoon salt

Turn the currant or grape jelly out into a deep plate and beat it to a foam. Then add dry mustard and salt and beat again thoroughly.

Cut steak with the grain on both sides of the bone, and give a strip from each side to every guest.

In carving a rolled roast of beef, hold it with the fork and slice it evenly across the grain.

*First cut off the legs and wings of a turkey or other large bird,
then slice the breast downward.*

*Meat pies are cut in wedge-shaped sections. A dinner knife
may be used, with a cold meat fork for serving.*

ENTRÉES AND MADE-OVER DISHES

PATTY CASES

Roll puff-paste to the thickness of one-half inch, and shape into circles two and one-half to three inches in diameter, with a cooky-cutter. Remove centers from one-half of these circles, using a smaller cutter. Brush the edges of the uncut circles with water, and fit on to them the rings, forming a little wall and leaving a cavity in the center. Chill thoroughly before baking in a hot oven. These shells may be prepared the day before and reheated when needed. The small centers removed from the puff-paste circles should also be baked and used as lids to the patties when finished.

BOUCHÉES

Small pastry shells or cases filled with creamed meat or game are called bouchées, and are much in vogue for entrées. They provide an excellent way of utilizing left-overs of chicken, sweetbreads, fish. Paper cases, bought at the confectioner's, may be used instead of the pastry shells.

TIMBALE CASES

1 teaspoon sugar	1 tablespoon oil
1/2 teaspoon salt	1/2 cup milk
3/4 cup flour	Fat for frying
1 egg	

Mix sugar, salt and sifted flour. Add the well-beaten egg, oil and milk. Beat with an egg-beater until perfectly smooth, then strain. This should be made an hour before it is needed and set aside in a cool place to lose the air which has been beaten into it. Pour into a cup that is deep enough to allow the timbale iron to be lowered into it to the required depth without touching the bottom.

71

Have ready a kettle of fat, place the iron in it and heat until the fat is hot enough to brown a piece of bread while counting forty. The fat should be deep enough to more than cover the mold end of the iron. When the iron is heated, take out, remove surplus fat, using crumpled tissue-paper, and lower into batter until iron is covered to not more than three-fourths of its height. This is necessary to allow for the rise of the batter in cooking. If only a thin layer of the batter adheres to the mold, dip it into the batter again until there is a smooth layer of the partly cooked batter. Plunge quickly into hot fat and cook for about twelve seconds.

When properly cooked, the timbale case should slip easily from the mold. Place the finished case on absorbent paper to drain and continue the operation until the required number are made. A fluted timbale iron is easier to work with, as the case does not slip off until thoroughly cooked. If the cases are not crisp, the batter is too thick and should be diluted with milk. These cases may be used with great variety. They may be filled with a choice creamed vegetable, or with creamed oysters, chicken or sweetbreads, or they may be filled with fresh or cooked fruit topped with whipped cream or powdered sugar, and served as a sweet course.

POTATO BORDER

9 medium-sized potatoes	1 tablespoon salt
2 tablespoons butter	2 eggs
½ cup hot milk	

Wash the potatoes, boil, drain, dry off and put through the ricer. Add butter, hot milk, salt and the well-beaten yolks of the eggs. Beat till very light. Pack into a border mold rubbed with butter, and let it stand away from the heat for eight minutes. Beat the whites of the two eggs to a froth and add one-fourth teaspoon of salt, turn the border on a warm platter, cover it with the beaten white, and brown in a moderate oven. Put meat or fish, heated in sauce, in the center.

RISSOLES

These are practically little turnovers, filled with a highly seasoned mixture of chopped chicken and ham or other delicate meat moistened with white sauce. Roll puff-paste very thin and cut in circles. Place a teaspoon of the mixture in the center of each circle, moisten half the circumference with cold water, and fold the other half over, pressing the edges closely together. Dip in slightly beaten egg mixed with a tablespoon of water. Fry in deep fat, and drain thoroughly.

CHICKEN PATTIES

For the filling, use equal quantities of button mushrooms and diced, cooked chicken mixed with one-half the quantity of medium white sauce. Heat thoroughly and put into the cases.

CLAM PATTIES

Fill patties with creamed clams.

LOBSTER PATTIES

Follow directions for the filling of chicken patties, substituting lobster for chicken.

SWEETBREAD PATTIES

Follow directions for the filling of chicken patties, substituting prepared sweetbreads for chicken.

MINCED CHICKEN WITH MUSHROOMS

2 cups cooked chicken, fresh or canned	½ teaspoon salt
	1 tablespoon butter
1 cup mushrooms	1 tablespoon flour
½ cup milk	¼ teaspoon pepper

Chop chicken moderately fine. Cut mushrooms into small pieces, boil them in their own liquor for five minutes, then skim them out and set aside to keep hot. Combine mushroom liquor and milk, make a white sauce with this liquid and the fat rubbed with the flour. Add mushrooms and chopped chicken, and cook three minutes, stirring continually. Add seasonings and serve on toast.

CREAMED SWEETBREADS

1 pair sweetbreads	1 cup milk or cream
1 tablespoon butter	Salt and pepper
1 tablespoon flour	1 tablespoon parsley

Prepare the sweetbreads and break them into small pieces. Make a white sauce, add the sweetbreads, and as soon as they are heated, season. Serve in pastry shells or on toast.

SWEETBREAD AND OYSTER PIE

1 pair sweetbreads
2 dozen oysters
1 tablespoon butter
1 tablespoon flour

1 cup cream or milk
2 egg-yolks, hard cooked
Pepper and salt
Puff or plain pie-paste

Prepare sweetbreads. Make a white sauce with fat, flour, cream or milk, and add the egg-yolks, chopped very fine. Add sweetbreads and prepared oysters to the sauce. Season, put in a deep baking-dish, cover with a layer of paste, and bake.

PREPARING PEPPERS FOR STUFFING

Cut off the tops of the peppers or cut them in two lengthwise, and remove the inner fibers and seeds. Drop into boiling water, remove from the fire, let stand ten to twelve minutes, then drain.

PEPPERS WITH MEAT STUFFING

6 green peppers
1 cup cooked meat, chopped fine

½ cup bread- or cracker-crums
Milk or cream

Prepare peppers as directed. Mix the meat with the bread or cracker-crums and moisten with a little milk or cream. Be sure that it is rather highly seasoned. (The potted meats that come in cans are excellent for this purpose.) Fill the peppers with the mixture and serve at once or cover with buttered crums and brown in the oven.

PEPPERS WITH CHEESE STUFFING

6 green peppers
1 cup crums
½ cup chopped cheese

1 tablespoon melted butter
Salt

Prepare peppers as directed. Mix the crums with the cheese. Then add the butter and salt to taste. Fill the peppers with the mixture and serve with the meat course.

SWEETBREADS IN PEPPER CASES

1 cup cooked sweetbreads
6 peppers
2 tablespoons butter
2 tablespoons flour
Crums

½ cup brown or white stock
(preferably chicken)
2 tablespoons cream
½ cup button mushrooms
Worcestershire sauce
Salt, pepper and paprika

Prepare the sweetbreads. Melt fat, add flour, salt and pepper. Mix smooth, add stock and cream. Cook until thick. Stir in the sweetbreads and mushrooms cut into small pieces and the seasoning. Fill prepared peppers, cover with buttered crums and bake. Mushroom sauce may be poured around the peppers.

SALMON CROQUETTES

1¾ cups cooked salmon, fresh
or canned
2 tablespoons butter
⅓ cup flour
1 cup milk

Salt and pepper
Cayenne
1 teaspoon lemon-juice
Egg and crums

Make a white sauce with the fat, flour and milk. Add salt, a little white pepper, and a few grains of cayenne. To this cream foundation add cold flaked salmon and lemon-juice. Spread on a plate to cool. Shape, dip in fine crums, roll in egg and again in crums and fry in deep fat.

SURPRISE CROQUETTES

2 cups mashed potatoes
4 tablespoons cream
1 teaspoon onion-juice
2 egg-yolks

1 egg-white
Salt and pepper
Cooked meat, cheese or
vegetable
Crums and flour

To the mashed potato add cream or rich milk, onion-juice and salt and pepper to taste. Beat over the fire until smooth and hot. Remove, slightly cool, and add the beaten egg-yolks. Form into cylinders, or cone shapes; make a depression in each, and into this put a teaspoon of creamed chicken, minced highly seasoned meat, grated cheese, or a vegetable in cream sauce. Press the potato around the filling. Beat the egg slightly, dilute, roll the croquettes in flour, egg and then in seasoned bread-crumbs, and fry in deep fat.

CHEESE CROQUETTES

3 tablespoons fat
3 tablespoons flour
⅔ cup milk
2 egg-yolks
1 cup cubes fresh mild cheese

½ cup grated Parmesan **or**
    Gruyère cheese
Paprika
Salt
Egg and crums

Make a thick white sauce with the fat, flour and milk. Add the yolks of eggs. Into this sauce stir the grated cheese, and, as soon as it melts, add the cheese cubes. Season with paprika and salt. Pour into a well-greased shallow pan to cool. When perfectly firm cut in any shape desired—circles, squares or strips—dip in fine crums, egg and again in crums. Fry in deep fat and drain on brown paper.

CHICKEN CROQUETTES

2 tablespoons butter
½ cup flour
1 cup milk
1¾ cups cooked fowl
Salt and pepper

¼ teaspoon celery salt
1 teaspoon lemon-juice
Few drops onion-juice
1 teaspoon chopped parsley
Egg and crums

Make a white sauce with the fat, flour and milk. Add fowl, seasoned with celery salt, lemon-juice, onion-juice, parsley, and salt and pepper. Cool, shape, dip in flour or fine crums, egg and crums, and fry in deep fat. White meat of fowl absorbs more sauce than dark meat.

HAM CROQUETTES

2 cups mashed potatoes
1 tablespoon butter or other
    fat
3 egg-yolks

Cayenne
1 cup cooked ham
Egg and crums

Mix potato, butter or other fat, yolks of two eggs and cayenne, beat until smooth, then set to cool. Chop the ham, mix with the other yolk, set on the stove for a moment, then turn out to cool. When thoroughly cool, take a tablespoon of the potato mixture, make a hole in it, put a large teaspoon of the chopped ham inside, close the hole and shape in a ball. Dip in flour, then in egg, roll in crums, and fry in deep fat.

CHEESE CUTLETS

1 ounce grated Parmesan cheese
3 egg-yolks
1 tablespoon cream

Mace
Salt
Cayenne
1 tablespoon thick white sauce

To the well-beaten egg-yolks, add cream and grated Parmesan cheese, and season with mace, cayenne and salt. Beat until very light and add the thick white sauce. Pour into a shallow greased pan and steam over hot water until firm. When cold, cut in shapes with a fancy cutter, dredge with grated cheese and fry in deep fat to a delicate brown. Serve at once on fried bread.

CHICKEN CUTLETS

2 cups cooked chicken
4 tablespoons chopped mushrooms
1 teaspoon salt
½ teaspoon pepper
1 teaspoon parsley
½ teaspoon onion-juice

1 tablespoon lemon-juice
2 tablespoons butter or other fat
1 tablespoon flour
1 cup milk or cream
4 eggs

Mix the chicken, mushrooms, salt, pepper, parsley and the onion and lemon-juice. Make a white sauce with the fat, flour and milk or cream. Add the chicken, and cook for three minutes. Stir in two of the eggs beaten until light. Take from the fire immediately, pour into a greased, flat dish and set in a cold place for an hour or so. The colder the mixture becomes, the better it may be handled. Shape into cutlets, either in molds or with a knife, and sprinkle both sides of each cutlet with fine crums. Beat the other two eggs in deep plates. Dip the cutlets in the egg, then in crums, put them in a frying-basket, not crowding them and cook in deep fat for two minutes. Serve with Béchamel or mushroom sauce.

SALMON CUTLETS

1 cup hot mashed potatoes
1 cup flaked salmon
Egg and crums

Salt and pepper
1 teaspoon lemon-juice

Add potato to salmon. Season with salt, pepper and lemon-juice. Shape into cutlets, egg and crum and fry in deep fat.

RICE FAN-TAN

½ cup rice
2 cups milk
½ teaspoon salt
2 tablespoons sugar

1 egg
½ cup candied fruits
Egg and crums
Powdered sugar

Cook rice in milk until very soft. Stir in salt, sugar and well-beaten egg, and remove at once from the fire. Mix in assorted candied fruits—cherries, apricots and pineapple—and turn into a shallow, well-oiled pan to cool. When firm, cut into strips about one and one-half inches wide and three inches long, dip in egg and bread-crums and brown delicately on both sides in butter or butter substitute. Drain, dust with powdered sugar and serve hot.

FRITTER BATTER

1½ cups flour
¼ teaspoon salt
2 teaspoons baking-powder

1 egg
⅔ cup milk
2 tablespoons powdered sugar
(for sweet fritters only)

Sift dry ingredients, add egg, well beaten, and milk. The batter should be thick enough to completely coat the article it is intended to cover. If too thin, add more flour. If too thick, add more liquid.

APPLE FRITTERS

1 cup milk
2 eggs
1 teaspoon sugar
Salt

2 cups flour
1 tablespoon baking-powder
Apples

To the milk add the well-beaten egg-yolks and the sugar, then the flour mixed and sifted with the baking-powder and the salt. Then fold in the stiffly beaten whites. Add sliced sour apples, being careful to get the batter all over them. Drop by spoonfuls into deep fat and fry.

BANANA FRITTERS

6 bananas
2 tablespoons sugar

3 tablespoons orange-juice
Fritter batter

Peel bananas, cut each in two and split each half. Place the pieces in a bowl with sugar and orange-juice and let them stand for one hour. Drain the fruit, dip in batter and fry in deep fat.

CORN FRITTERS

2 cups corn, fresh or canned	1 teaspoon melted butter
1 teaspoon salt	½ cup milk
⅛ teaspoon pepper	2 cups flour
1 egg	1 teaspoon baking-powder

Chop the corn very fine and add salt, pepper, well-beaten egg, butter, milk, flour and baking-powder. Fry in deep fat.

CLAM FRITTERS

24 soft clams	1 cup milk
2 cups flour	½ cup clam liquor
1 teaspoon baking-powder	2 eggs
½ teaspoon salt	Salt and pepper

Make a batter of flour, baking-powder, salt, milk, clam liquor and well-beaten eggs. Chop two dozen soft clams, season with salt and pepper, add to the batter and drop by tablespoonfuls into deep fat.

CHICKEN A LA KING

2½ cups diced cooked chicken	1 minced green pepper
2 tablespoons butter	2 chopped pimentos
2 tablespoons flour	4 or 5 chopped olives
2 cups milk	1 teaspoon salt
1 cup cream or evaporated milk	½ teaspoon paprika
	¼ teaspoon white pepper

Scald milk and cream, add seasonings. Melt butter and add flour to make a smooth paste. Take milk from fire and cool slightly. Add flour and butter mixture and beat. Cook over hot water until creamy. Add olives, peppers and chicken and stir while cooking. Serve on hot toast, in croustades or in patty shells.

VEGETARIAN DISHES

CHESTNUT CROQUETTES

2 cups hot mashed chestnuts
4 tablespoons butter or other fat
Salt and pepper

2 eggs
Few drops onion-juice or 2 tablespoons finely chopped onion
Egg and crums

Mix the chestnuts, butter, slightly beaten eggs and seasonings. Shape into croquettes. Roll in crums, beaten egg and crums. Fry in deep hot fat until crums are brown.

This offers an adequate protein, iron and a comparatively highly seasoned dish. The croquettes may be served with brown sauce or tomato sauce.

PEANUT-BUTTER CUTLETS

1½ cups peanut butter
1½ cups hot milk
6 half-inch slices of bread

1 teaspoon salt
Pepper

Mix peanut butter with hot milk and seasoning, mixing together thoroughly. Dip slices of bread into the peanut-butter mixture. Sauté in hot fat. Garnish with pickles and olives.

This dish offers both adequate protein and iron.

PEANUT SOUFFLÉ

1 tablespoon butter
6 tablespoons flour
¾ cup peanut butter
1½ teaspoons salt

Few drops lemon-juice
1½ cups scalded milk
4 eggs

Melt the butter and add the flour, peanut butter and seasoning. Cook for three minutes, stirring constantly. Add scalded milk, and continue cooking until the mixture reaches the boiling-point.

*Cold boiled salmon with green mayonnaise and cucumber fingers.
Served with cold boiled peas and French dressing.*

*Tomato jelly in a ring mold filled with hearts of lettuce, hard
cooked eggs and mayonnaise. Garnished with cheese balls and
Roquefort cheese wedges.*

Pear Conde combines rice and fruit in a dessert to delight the epicure. The recipe is on page 166.

Sandwich spreads and cheeses in interesting packages.

Here is inspiration for the sandwich maker.

Remove from the fire, pour the hot mixture over the well-beaten egg-yolks, mixing them in well. Cool, and fold in the egg-whites that have been beaten until stiff and dry. When the ingredients are thoroughly combined, place in a baking-dish, set in a pan of water in a moderate oven (350° F.), and bake thirty minutes. Serve immediately.

This dish is a good luncheon dish but, because of its texture, should have something crisp or solid served with it.

MOCK SAUSAGE

1 cup dried Lima beans or 3 cups cooked beans of any kind
⅔ cup bread-crums

3 eggs
2 tablespoons butter
½ teaspoon sage
Salt and pepper

Pick over and wash beans, cover with water and let soak overnight. Drain, cook in boiling salted water until tender, then force through a strainer. Add remaining ingredients, shape into form of sausages, roll in crums, egg, and crums again. Sauté until brown. Serve with tomato sauce.

This recipe makes six to eight sausages, three inches long and three-fourths of an inch thick. It should be accompanied by some milk, egg or cheese dish.

BEAN ROAST

1 cup well-roasted shelled peanuts
2 cups well-seasoned mashed potatoes
2 cups cooked Lima beans, fresh or canned

¼ cup milk
1 egg
1 teaspoon salt
⅛ teaspoon paprika
1 teaspoon onion-juice

Grind the peanuts, using the finest blade of the food-chopper. In a well-oiled baking-dish place a layer of potatoes, a layer of beans and a layer of peanuts. Continue making layers until all the ingredients are used. Blend milk with well-beaten egg and seasoning and pour over the top. Bake in a moderate oven (350° F.) until brown. Serve with brown sauce or tomato sauce.

VEGETABLE LUNCHEON

1 pound kidney beans
1 cup diced carrot
1 green pepper
1 large onion

2 cups cooked tomatoes, **fresh** or canned
½ cup rice
½ dozen large mushrooms

Soak the beans in cold water overnight. Drain and cook in boiling water slowly for about four hours. A ham-bone or a piece of bacon cooked with them adds to the flavor. Drain, and add chopped carrots, pepper, thinly sliced onion and tomatoes. Simmer until tender. Boil rice separately in salted water, drain and add to the vegetables. (The rice water should be saved to use in soups or gravies.) Garnish with sautéd green peppers and mushrooms.

Serve with some milk, egg or cheese dish.

CELERY, NUT AND POTATO LOAF

2 large stalks celery
¾ cup chopped nuts
3 cups mashed potatoes
3 tablespoons fat

1 egg
1 teaspoon salt
⅛ teaspoon paprika
2 teaspoons grated onion

Wash, cut in small pieces and cook the celery in a small amount of boiling salted water until it is tender. Drain off liquid. (This may be used for soup stock later.) Then add the other ingredients in the order in which they are given. Combine them carefully, pack in a loaf in a well-oiled bread-pan, and bake in a moderate oven (350° F.) for thirty-five minutes. Serve with tomato sauce.

An adequate protein is needed as accompaniment to this dish.

NUT LOAF

2 cups soft bread-crums
1 cup milk
2 cups chopped nut-meats

2 eggs
1 teaspoon salt
1 teaspoon paprika

Soak bread-crums in milk, add nuts, slightly beaten eggs and seasonings. Turn into greased bread-pan, set in pan of water and bake forty minutes. Serve with tomato sauce. The loaf may be steamed instead of baked.

For luncheon the table is more informal than for dinner, but beauty and orderliness are indispensable to the charm of your table

This tea-table, in the dining-room of the Delineator Home Institute, shows the beauty of linen and silver

When the finger-bowl is brought in on the dessert plate, it is equally correct to use or omit a doily

BOSTON ROAST

1½ cups dry kidney beans
3 tablespoons salt
1 to 2 cups grated cheese

2 tablespoons chopped onion
1 cup bread-crums
½ cup milk

Soak beans twenty-four hours. Cook until soft in water in which the salt has been dissolved. Drain, chop, add onion, cheese, crums, more salt if needed, and enough milk to moisten. Form into a loaf. Bake in a moderate oven (350° F.) for forty minutes. Baste occasionally with hot water and fat.

COTTAGE-CHEESE AND PEANUT LOAF

½ cup peanuts
1 cup cottage cheese
1 cup cold, cooked rolled oats
1 cup milk
1 egg, slightly beaten
1 tablespoon fat

½ teaspoon salt
Dash of pepper
1 teaspoon poultry seasoning
Few drops Worcestershire sauce
1 tablespoon chopped onion

Chop peanuts and add to other ingredients in order given. When thoroughly combined, place in a well-oiled bread-tin. Bake in a moderate oven (350° F.) until brown. Serve hot with tomato sauce.

NUT AND CHEESE LOAF

1 tablespoon chopped onion
1 tablespoon fat
1 cup grated cheese
1 cup chopped nuts
½ cup milk
1 cup cooked cereal
1 teaspoon salt

1 teaspoon sugar
¼ teaspoon paprika
1½ tablespoons lemon-juice
½ teaspoon Worcestershire sauce
Buttered crums

Cook onion in fat until delicately brown. Mix with all the other ingredients and moisten with milk. Cover with buttered crums and brown in oven. Serve hot with tomato sauce.

Serve with some crispy food, as celery.

EGG DISHES

EGG TOAST

6 slices toast   6 eggs
Butter   Salt and pepper

Moisten the edges of the toast with hot water and spread it with butter. Separate the yolks and whites of the eggs. Poach the yolks in salted water until soft cooked, and place one on each slice of toast, being careful not to break it. Beat the whites until very stiff, spread in circles around the yolks, season with salt and pepper, and brown in the oven. Serve hot.

EGGS IN BROWN BUTTER

6 eggs   Salt and pepper
3 tablespoons butter   1 teaspoon vinegar

Sauté the eggs in one tablespoon butter until set, season with salt and pepper, and place on a platter. Brown two tablespoons butter in the pan, add one teaspoon vinegar, and when hot, pour over the eggs.

BAKED EGGS, OR "EGGS SUR LE PLAT"

Use individual baking-dishes and melt one teaspoon of butter in each dish. Break the eggs into the dishes, allowing one or two eggs to a dish. Sprinkle with salt and pepper, and place a tiny piece of butter on each. Bake in a moderate oven (350° F.) until the eggs are set but not hard. Serve in the baking-dishes.

BAKED EGGS IN TOMATO SAUCE

12 tablespoons thick tomato   6 tablespoons grated cheese
    soup   Salt and pepper
6 poached eggs

Grease small ramekins and place two tablespoons tomato sauce in each. Lay a poached egg in each dish, cover with grated cheese, season with salt and pepper, and bake in a quick oven (two or three minutes) to brown the cheese. The oven must be very hot, as the cheese should be nicely colored while the eggs are still soft and creamy.

EGGS IN BACON RINGS

6 long slices of bacon	Salt and pepper
6 eggs	Garnish of parsley

Curl slices of bacon around the inside of muffin-cups or small ramekins. Break an egg inside each bacon-ring, season with salt and pepper and bake until set, but not hard. Remove carefully from the dish so that the egg will remain fastened to the bacon. Arrange on a platter and garnish with parsley.

EGGS À LA SUISSE

6 eggs	1 cup cream
2 tablespoons butter	Salt
½ to 1 cup grated cheese	Cayenne

Spread the bottom of a baking-dish with butter. Sprinkle a layer of grated cheese over it and break the eggs on the cheese, being careful not to break the yolks. Pour a little cream over the eggs, then more grated cheese. Season with salt and cayenne, and bake in a moderate oven (350° F.) until the eggs are set, but not hard. Serve in the baking-dish.

BAKED EGGS ESPAGNOLE

6 eggs	4 tablespoons butter
3 tablespoons chopped onion	¼ cup bread-crums
3 tablespoons chopped green pepper	½ cup grated cheese

Fry onion and pepper in the butter until slightly brown, then pour into a baking-dish. Break the eggs into the dish, being careful not to break the yolks. Mix the crums with the cheese and sprinkle over the eggs. Bake in a moderate oven (350° F.) until the eggs are set, but not hard. Serve in the dish in which they were baked.

PLANKED EGGS

1 cup finely chopped cooked
  ham or corned beef
1 cup crums
Cream

6 poached eggs
Garnish of tomato slices
Green-pepper rings
1 quart mashed potato

Mix the meat with the crums and enough cream to make a paste.
Spread the mixture on a heated plank of suitable size. Around
the edge of the plank make a narrow border of mashed potato
and inside the border make six nests of the potato. Slip a poached
egg into each nest and set in the oven until the potato turns a
delicate brown. Garnish with alternate slices of tomato and
green-pepper rings.

BATTERED OR SCRAMBLED EGGS

In a frying-pan, place one tablespoon of butter for each egg
to be used. Beat the eggs until the whites and yolks are well
mixed. Season with salt and pepper and add one to three tablespoons of milk or cream for each egg. Pour into the hot fat and
cook slowly, stirring constantly until the eggs are of the desired
consistency. Serve at once. A little onion-juice or chopped parsley may be added to the eggs, if desired. Eggs cooked in this
way in the top of a double boiler will be more creamy than those
cooked in a frying-pan.

EGGS IN TOMATOES

1 small onion
2 cups tomato
1 teaspoon salt

1/4 teaspoon pepper
6 eggs
Toast

Cut the onion into small pieces and place with the tomato in a
shallow pan. Stew very slowly for ten minutes. Add salt and
pepper, then reduce the heat until the tomato stops bubbling.
Break the eggs and slip them on top of the tomato, being careful
not to break the yolks. Cook slowly until the whites of the
eggs are set, then prick the yolks and let them mingle with the
tomato and the whites. The mixture should be quite soft, but the
red tomatoes should be quite distinct. Serve at once on buttered
toast.

CUBAN EGGS

6 eggs
¼ cup sausage meat
1 teaspoon chopped onion

½ teaspoon salt
Pepper

Cook the meat and onion together for five minutes. Beat the eggs until light, add the seasonings, and pour into the pan with the meat. Cook slowly, stirring constantly, until the eggs are thick and creamy. Serve with buttered toast or poured over slices of toast.

EGGS À LA CARACAS

1 tablespoon butter
¼ pound dried beef
1 tablespoon grated cheese
1 cup tomatoes

Salt and pepper
4 eggs
Onion-juice

Melt the butter in a frying-pan and, when hot, add the dried beef and cheese. Toss lightly until the beef is slightly frizzled, add the tomatoes, the seasonings, and the eggs beaten until light. Stir and cook gently until of a creamy consistency.

PLAIN PUFFY OMELET

4 eggs
4 tablespoons hot water

2 tablespoons cooked tapioca
Salt and pepper
Butter

Beat the egg-whites until stiff. Beat the yolks until thick and lemon-colored, beat into them the hot water and add salt and pepper. Cut and fold together the yolks and stiffly beaten whites. Melt enough butter in an omelet-pan to grease the bottom and sides of the pan. Turn the egg mixture into the pan and cook over a slow fire until it is puffy and a light brown underneath, then place in the oven until the top is dry. Touch the top of the omelet lightly with the finger and if the egg does not stick to the finger the omelet is done. Do not overcook it or it will shrink or be tough.

Loosen the edges of the omelet, slip a spatula or flexible knife under the side next to the handle of the pan, fold one-half over the other and press slightly to make it stay in place, slip on to a hot plate and serve at once. Tapioca keeps omelet from falling.

PLAIN FRENCH OMELET

6 eggs   2 tablespoons butter
Salt and pepper

Beat the eggs just enough to mix the whites and yolks, and add salt and pepper. Heat butter in an omelet-pan, pour a little of it into the beaten eggs and allow the remainder to get hot. Turn the eggs into the pan and as the mixture cooks on the bottom and sides, prick it with a fork so that the egg on top will penetrate the cooked surface, and run under the sides. The work must be done quickly and carefully so that the eggs are not all stirred up like scrambled eggs. While the eggs are still soft, but slightly thickened, fold over, let stand a few minutes to brown, and turn on to a hot dish.

VARIATIONS OF PLAIN OMELET

Variations of the plain puffy omelet or the plain French omelet may be made by adding any of the following ingredients to the omelet before it is put into the pan to cook, or by spreading one of them on top just before the omelet is folded. Allow one tablespoon of mixture to each two eggs used.

Fish—Use any cooked fish. Chop it fine, season with salt and pepper and moisten with a little cream. Spread on the omelet before folding.

Ham or other meat—Scatter finely chopped meat over the center of the omelet while it is cooking. The meat may be improved by browning in a small amount of fat before it is added.

Cheese or parsley—Prepare as for ham omelet.

Onion—Mix one tablespoon chopped onion and one teaspoon chopped parsley. Add to the omelet mixture before cooking.

Jelly—Spread any jelly or jam over the omelet just before folding.

OYSTER OMELET

12 oysters   1 cup cream
½ tablespoon flour   6 eggs
2 tablespoons butter   Salt and pepper

Chop the oysters. Make a sauce of the flour, butter and the cream. Add the well-beaten eggs, season with salt and pepper, stir in the oysters and cook as a plain omelet.

What could be more tempting than a salad of greens, such as endive, chicory and lettuce?

To turn an egg salad into a daisy salad, use the whites as petals and make centers of the yolks.

Asparagus salad, with pepper rings as garnish, is shown above separated for easy serving.

The alligator pear, or avocado, requires the simplest of dressings when served as a salad.

EGG TIMBALES

1 tablespoon butter	3 eggs
1 tablespoon flour	Salt and pepper
⅔ cup scalded milk	Cayenne
1 tablespoon chopped parsley	Celery salt

Make a white sauce of the butter, flour, and milk, and add the egg-yolks, slightly beaten. Add all the seasonings, then fold in the stiffly beaten egg-whites. Fill greased baking-dishes two-thirds full of the mixture. Set dishes in a pan of hot water and poach in a moderate oven (350° F.) until firm. Arrange on a platter and serve with tomato cream sauce.

PICNIC EGGS (DEVILED)

Mash the yolks of hard-cooked eggs, season with salt, pepper, butter, a little mustard and vinegar. Minced potted ham may be added, or the yolks may be mixed with mayonnaise dressing. Refill the whites with the mixture, press two halves together and wrap each egg in a square of oiled paper, the ends of which are twisted to keep the halves in place.

SAVORY EGGS

6 hot hard-cooked eggs	Chopped parsley
Salt and pepper	Anchovy paste
¼ cup hot cream	6 slices hot buttered toast
1 cup hot thin white sauce	

Cut the eggs in two lengthwise and remove the yolks. Mash the yolks, add seasonings, cream, parsley, anchovy or any desired relish, and refill the whites. Place on slices of toast and pour the white sauce over them.

EGGS À LA GOLDENROD

6 hard-cooked eggs	Salt and pepper
2 cups thin white sauce	Paprika
8 slices toast	

Separate the yolks from the whites of the eggs and chop the whites very fine. Add to the white sauce with salt, pepper, paprika. Arrange six slices of toast on a platter and pour over them the white sauce mixture. Press the egg-yolks through a sieve and scatter over the top. Cut the two extra slices of toast into small triangles, or points, arrange on the platter and garnish with parsley.

EGGS AU GRATIN

6 hard-cooked eggs	Grated cheese
Salt and pepper	Buttered crums
2 cups medium white, tomato or yellow sauce	Butter

Remove the shells from the eggs, slice them and arrange in a greased baking-dish. Season with salt and pepper and pour the sauce over them. Yellow sauce may be made from white sauce by adding uncooked beaten egg-yolk to white sauce. Sprinkle with grated cheese and cover with buttered crums. Bake in a moderate oven until the sauce bubbles and the crums brown.

CHEESE DISHES

WELSH RABBIT

1 tablespoon butter	¼ teaspoon mustard
1 tablespoon flour	¼ to 1 pound of cheese
1 cup milk	(acccording to richness de-
½ teaspoon salt	sired) shaved or cut fine
Few grains pepper	6 slices buttered toast

Make a white sauce, in the top of a double boiler, of the first six ingredients, mixing the mustard with the other dry ingredients. Set the top part of the boiler over hot but not boiling water. Add the cheese, cook and stir until it is melted. Serve on hot toasted bread or on saltines. One-half cup chopped olives may be added. This dish may be varied by adding one or two slightly beaten eggs just after the cheese has melted and continuing the cooking until the egg has thickened the mixture.

MEXICAN RABBIT

½ tablespoon butter	¼ teaspoon salt
½ green pepper	½ cup canned tomatoes
2 cups grated cheese	½ cup bread-crumbs
1 egg	6 slices buttered toast
1 cup canned corn	

Melt the butter in the top of the double boiler, add the chopped pepper and cook until slightly softened, but not browned. Set over hot water, add the cheese and stir constantly until the cheese is melted. Mix beaten egg, salt and corn and stir into the cheese mixture; add the chopped tomatoes and crums. Heat the mixture and serve on toasted bread.

CHEESE FONDUE

1 cup grated cheese	⅓ teaspoon salt
2 teaspoons butter	3 eggs
1 cup milk	Cayenne
1 cup soft bread-crumbs	

Scald the milk and pour it over the crums, then add the butter or butter substitute, the cheese and seasonings. Beat the egg-yolks slightly and add to the mixture, then fold in the stiffly beaten whites and turn the mixture into a greased baking-dish. Set in a pan of water and bake in a slow oven (300° F.) until firm on top.

One cup of cooked rice or other cereal may be substituted for the bread-crums.

CHEESE SOUFFLÉ

1 cup cheese	4 tablespoons butter, or other fat
3 eggs	
1 cup milk	½ teaspoon salt
4 tablespoons flour	Pepper

Make a white sauce of milk, flour, fat and seasonings. Add the cheese and beaten egg-yolks and stir until the cheese has melted and the yolks are set. Fold in stiffly beaten egg-whites. Pour into a buttered dish, or buttered individual molds, and set in a pan of hot water. Bake fifteen minutes in a slow oven (300° F.), or until the egg-white is set, and serve at once. It begins to fall as soon as removed from oven.

The cheese soufflé may be baked in ramekin dishes and served as a cheese course for dinner.

LUNCHEON CHEESE AND EGGS

1 cup cream	2 tablespoons grated cheese
6 eggs	Salt and pepper

Put the cream into a frying-pan and let it heat to the boiling-point, then break in, carefully, the eggs. Lower the heat under the eggs and cook until they are set, as in poaching, spooning the cream over the top of the eggs while they are cooking. Put them on a hot platter. To the cream left in the frying-pan, add the grated cheese and seasonings. Stir until melted and pour the mixture over the eggs.

VEGETABLES

ASPARAGUS

Trim stalks to uniform length, wash and tie with soft string. Cook in boiling water until tender, keeping the tips above the water for the first ten minutes. Just before cooking is completed, salt the water. Drain, untie, and season with melted butter or butter substitute, salt and pepper.

If preferred, the asparagus may be cut into inch pieces. In this case, the stalks are put into the water ten minutes or more before the tips are added. Asparagus may be served with medium white sauce or Hollandaise sauce may be poured over it.

FRENCH ARTICHOKES

The artichoke consists of three parts: the bottom, the leaves and the choke. The choke is not eaten and may be removed or not, as preferred. If it is to be removed, cut out the stem and save it; then with the point of a sharp knife cut around the base of the choke and draw out the latter. Cut across the top of the artichoke to trim it. Then wash it and soak it for half an hour in salted water, using one tablespoon of salt to two quarts of water.

After removing the choke and soaking as directed, press the stem back into the head, lay the whole head downward in a kettle and cover with boiling water, adding one teaspoon of salt and two teaspoons of lemon-juice for every two quarts of water. Boil gently until tender. Then take the artichoke from the water and drain. Serve hot with Béchamel sauce or Hollandaise sauce, or cold with a French dressing or well-seasoned mayonnaise dressing, or with Russian dressing.

BOSTON BAKED BEANS

1 pint pea beans	½ teaspoon salt
1 small onion	½ teaspoon dry mustard
⅛ pound salt pork, part fat and part lean	2 tablespoons molasses

Soak beans in cold water overnight; in the morning place them in fresh water to cover and simmer gently until skins begin to burst, being careful that they do not cook long enough to break. When they are soft turn them into a bean-pot. Beans may be put into the pot without this preliminary cooking.

Pour boiling water over the salt pork. Scrape the rind until white, score it in half-inch strips, and bury the meat in the beans, leaving only the rind exposed. Mix together salt, mustard and molasses. Place these in a cup, fill the cup with hot water, stir until well mixed, and pour the liquid over the beans and pork. Add enough water to cover the beans, and bake eight hours, adding water to keep them covered, until the last hour, when the pork should be raised to the surface to crisp.

If pork is disliked, it may be omitted, but more salt must then be used, together with one-third cup of butter or butter substitute or drippings, or half a pound of fat and lean corned beef may be substituted.

BEETS

Wash the beets thoroughly and remove the leaves, being very careful not to break off the little fibers and rootlets which retain the juices and coloring matter. Use plenty of water in cooking. Should the beets be tough and withered, soak them for twenty-four hours in plenty of cold water before trying to cook them.

Try with a fork, and when tender drop them into a pan of cold water and slip off the skins with the hands. If small, serve whole. If large, slice those to be used immediately, place in a dish and season with salt, pepper, and butter or butter substitute or savory fat. A teaspoon of sugar may be added also if the beets are not naturally sweet enough. Set them over boiling water to heat thoroughly and serve hot, with or without vinegar. The cold beets left over may be covered with vinegar and used as pickles.

BRUSSELS SPROUTS

Pick off the dead leaves from the sprouts, soak the sprouts in cold salted water for one-half hour, wash them and put them on the fire in plenty of boiling water. Boil in an uncovered saucepan until tender. Just before they are done, salt the water. Drain in a colander. Reheat with melted butter or butter substitute, season with salt and pepper, and serve very hot. They may be served with cream sauce.

SCALLOPED CABBAGE WITH CHEESE

1 small head cabbage
2 cups grated cheese

1½ cup medium white sauce
½ to ¾ cup bread-crums

Shred the cabbage and cook for twenty minutes. Into a greased baking-dish, put a layer of cabbage, then a layer of cheese, then a layer of white sauce, and continue to add layers until the ingredients are all used. Cover the top of the mixture with the crums, which may be mixed with a little melted butter, and bake in a moderate oven (350° F.) for about twenty minutes, or until the crums are brown.

CARROTS AND PEAS

2 cups cubed carrots
1 cup cooked peas, fresh or canned
3 tablespoons butter
3 tablespoons flour

½ teaspoon salt
⅛ teaspoon pepper
2 teaspoons sugar
1½ cups milk

Boil the carrots until tender. Combine with the cooked peas, reheat and serve with melted butter or savory fat or make a sauce of the flour, fat, milk and seasonings, add the cooked carrots and peas, reheat and serve hot.

CARROTS AND PEAS WITH GREEN MINT

1 very small bunch fresh mint
2 cups cooked cubed carrots
1 cup cooked peas

Salt and pepper
Butter
Sugar

Boil together carrots, peas and mint leaves for five minutes. Drain, add salt and pepper, a generous amount of butter, and sprinkle with sugar. Set in the oven until the sugar melts. Serve with a garnish of fresh mint leaves.

SCALLOPED CAULIFLOWER WITH EGG

1 medium cauliflower
2 cooked eggs
Salt and pepper

1½ cups medium white sauce
Bread-crums

Break the head into small flowerets and cook in boiling water. Add salt just before cooking is completed. Drain. Grease a baking-dish and place a layer of cauliflower in it, then a layer of sliced eggs, then a layer of white sauce. Put a layer of crums over the top and bake in a hot oven until brown. Four table-spoons of grated cheese may be used instead of the hard-cooked eggs. A bit of cayenne pepper may be added for additional seasoning.

SCALLOPED CELERY WITH CHEESE

2 cups cooked celery cut into inch-long pieces
2 tablespoons butter
2 tablespoons flour
1 cup milk

Onion salt
Pepper
1 to 2 tablespoons grated cheese
Bread-crums

Make a sauce of the flour, fat, milk and seasonings. Put the celery into this and turn it into a greased ramekin or earthen pudding-dish. Sprinkle with cheese and bread-crums, mixed with a little butter, and bake until a golden brown. This is a simple but hearty dish.

CELERIAC

Not every housewife knows celeriac, but it is well worth adding to her list of vegetable acquaintances. It is a variety of celery grown for its turnip-like root instead of for the blanched stalks. The flavor is similar to that of celery. It is delicious served in various sauces or as a salad.

To prepare celeriac, trim off the tops, wash and pare the bulb, drop it into boiling water and cook about one-half hour, or until tender. Add the salt just before cooking is completed. It may then be prepared as stewed celery or scalloped celery with cheese.

CORN SOUFFLÉ

1 tablespoon butter or savory fat
1 tablespoon flour
½ cup milk
1 teaspoon salt
¼ teaspoon paprika

Pepper
1 pimiento
2 cups corn pulp (fresh or canned)
2 eggs

Make a white sauce, using the fat, flour, milk and seasoning. Rub the pimiento through a sieve and add it to the sauce. Add the corn to the mixture. Cool slightly, then add the well-beaten egg-yolks and fold in the stiffly beaten egg-whites. Turn into a greased baking-dish, set the dish in a pan of hot water, and bake in a moderate oven until the egg is set, about thirty minutes.

CORN OYSTERS

2 cups corn pulp

2 eggs

2 tablespoons flour

2 tablespoons butter or other fat

Salt and pepper

If fresh corn is used, grate it from the cob with a coarse grater. If canned corn is used, select one of the sieved varieties. Beat the egg-yolks and whites separately and add to the grated corn, with flour and butter or fat, salt and pepper. Drop the batter from a spoon into hot fat and fry light brown. Drain on soft paper. Serve hot.

DEVILED CORN

2 tablespoons butter or savory fat

2 tablespoons flour

1½ cups milk

1 teaspoon salt

¼ teaspoon mustard

Paprika

2 cups corn pulp (fresh or canned)

1 egg

1 tablespoon Worcestershire sauce

Crums

Make a sauce of the fat, flour and seasonings, add corn, egg slightly beaten, and Worcestershire sauce. Pour into a baking-dish, cover with crums mixed with a little butter or butter substitute and bake until crums are brown.

BAKED CORN AND TOMATOES

2 cups cooked corn (fresh or canned)

2 cups tomatoes (fresh or canned)

1 teaspoon salt

Pepper

1 teaspoon sugar

1 cup fresh bread-crums

3 tablespoons butter or savory fat

Mix seasonings with the corn and tomatoes and pour all into a greased baking-dish. Spread the crums over the top, dot them with the butter, and bake in a moderate oven for one-half hour. This is a satisfactory way of utilizing left-over corn or tomatoes.

CUCUMBER CUPS

This makes a dainty dish for luncheon. Cut the unpeeled vegetables into sections two inches long and cook until tender in water salted just before cooking is completed. Scoop out the center of each section, leaving one-half-inch thickness all around the sides, as well as on the bottom, thus making pretty green cups of the vegetable. These cups may be filled with creamed chicken, sweetbreads, mushrooms or any other filling, held together with white sauce.

STUFFED EGGPLANT

1 eggplant	½ cup water
2 tablespoons butter	2 cups crums
Salt and pepper	

Cut the eggplant in half lengthwise and scoop out the center pulp, leaving the rind about one-half inch thick so that the shape may be firm. Cover the shells with cold water. Chop the pulp fine, season it with salt and pepper, add butter or other savory fat and cook in a frying-pan for ten minutes, stirring well, then add water and one cup of bread-crums. Drain the shells, sprinkle the interior of each with salt and pepper and fill them with the mixture. Spread one cup of crums on the surface of the mixture, place the two pieces of plant in a baking-dish or deep pan, and pour enough hot water into the pan to come one-third up the sides of the plant. Bake one hour, and serve hot.

CREAMED KOHLRABI

6 kohlrabies	Salt
2 tablespoons butter or savory fat	Paprika
	2 cups milk
2 tablespoons flour	1 egg-yolk

Wash and pare the kohlrabies. Cut into half-inch cubes, drop into boiling water to cover and cook until tender. Just before cooking is completed, add salt, then drain and shake over the fire to dry slightly. Make a white sauce from the flour, fat, milk and seasonings, adding the egg-yolk last, and pour it over the vegetable.

SAUTÉD LENTILS

1 pint lentils
¼ teaspoon soda
Salt and pepper

2 tablespoons butter or savory fat

Wash the lentils and soak overnight. In the morning, drain them, cover with warm water in which the soda has been dissolved, and bring them quickly to the boiling-point. Boil gently for one hour, drain, cover them again with fresh boiling water, and boil gently until tender; this generally requires about one and one-half to two hours longer. Test by mashing a lentil between the fingers. If it crushes quickly, they are done. Drain in a colander.

Place butter or fat in a frying-pan and when it is melted add the lentils, with salt and pepper to season; stir them over the fire for fifteen minutes. Two minced onions may be added to the lentils, if desired.

MACÉDOINE OF VEGETABLES

2 cups mixed cooked vegetables
1 teaspoon beef extract or
   ½ cup stock
1 teaspoon sugar

½ cup water
Salt and pepper
2 tablespoons butter

Mix all the ingredients together and cook eight or ten minutes over a hot fire, shaking the pan now and then. Serve hot.

BAKED MACARONI OR SPAGHETTI WITH CHEESE

2 cups macaroni or spaghetti
   broken into short lengths
¼ pound grated cheese

2 tablespoons butter
1½ cups milk
Salt and pepper

Boil and drain the macaroni or spaghetti. Arrange a layer in the bottom of a pudding-dish. Over it sprinkle some of the cheese and scatter over this bits of butter or other fat. Add a sprinkling of salt and pepper. Fill the dish in this order, having macaroni on top, well oiled with butter, but without cheese. Add milk enough to just cover well and bake until a golden brown hue, one-half hour usually being sufficient. Serve in the dish in which it was baked.

MACARONI OR SPAGHETTI WITH TOMATO SAUCE

Break the macaroni or spaghetti into short lengths. Cover with plenty of boiling water and boil until soft, twenty to thirty minutes generally being required. Stir occasionally with a fork to prevent sticking to the kettle. Turn into a sieve and drain thoroughly. Place in the serving-dish and cover with tomato sauce. Serve grated cheese with it. This cheese may be mixed with the tomato sauce. Some people prefer spaghetti cooked in long pieces. To do this place the ends in boiling water and coil it as it softens.

STUFFED ONIONS

6 medium to large onions	½ cup milk
½ cup chopped ham or chopped green pepper	Pepper
	½ teaspoon salt
½ cup soft bread-crums	1 tablespoon fat
Fine dry bread-crums	

Remove a slice from the top of each onion and parboil the onions until almost tender. Drain and remove the centers, making six little cups. Chop the onion that was scooped out and combine with it the ham and soft crums. Add seasoning and refill the onion cups. Place them in a baking-dish, cover with crums, add the milk, and bake until tender.

STUFFED PEPPERS

6 green peppers	1 cup water or stock
½ onion	1¼ cups moistened bread-crums
1¼ cups cooked meat (veal, chicken or ham)	Salt and pepper
	1 tablespoon drippings or butter

Cut a slice from the stem end of each pepper. Remove seeds and parboil peppers ten minutes. Mix finely chopped cooked meat with moistened bread-crums, add salt, pepper and the onion, grated. Stuff the peppers with this mixture and stand them in a dripping-pan. Add water or stock. Bake fifteen minutes, basting frequently. Cooked rice may be used instead of the bread-crums.

SCALLOPED POTATOES

6 medium-sized potatoes	Milk
2 tablespoons flour	Salt and pepper
4 tablespoons butter	

Pare raw potatoes and cut them into thin slices. Place in a baking-dish a layer of the potato one inch deep, season with salt and pepper, sprinkle a portion of the flour over each layer, add a part of the butter or butter substitute in bits. Then add another layer of the potato and seasoning, as before, and continue until the required amount is used. It is advisable not to have more than two or three layers because of difficulty in cooking. Add milk until it can be seen between the slices of potato, cover and bake one and one-fourth hour, or until potatoes are tender when pierced with a fork, removing the cover during the last fifteen minutes to brown the top. Serve from the baking-dish.

FRANCONIA POTATOES

The potatoes should not be small, else they will bake dry and crusty. Pare the potatoes, boil them fifteen minutes, and drain well. Then place them in the baking-pan with the roast, and cook for forty-five minutes, turning often and basting with the gravy from the roast. Serve them arranged about the meat. Some cooks do not parboil the potatoes before putting them in the pan, but in that case a longer time is required for cooking.

POTATO PUFF OR SOUFFLÉ

2 cups hot mashed potatoes	2 tablespoons butter
2 eggs	1 cup milk

To the mashed potatoes add the fat, the egg-yolks which have been beaten until very light, and the milk. Stir until well blended and then fold in the stiffly beaten egg-whites. Mix lightly and pile the mass into a well-greased baking-dish. Bake in a moderate oven about ten minutes. Serve at once.

MASHED POTATOES AU GRATIN

6 potatoes riced	2 eggs
3 tablespoons butter	1/4 cup grated cheese
1/2 teaspoon salt	1/2 cup buttered crums
1/2 teaspoon paprika	

Add butter, seasoning and eggs to the hot riced potatoes. Beat until light and mound on a baking-dish. Cover with grated cheese and then with buttered crums to which the melted butter or butter substitute has been added.   Bake fifteen minutes, or until the crums are brown.

FRENCH FRIED POTATOES

Wash and pare potatoes and cut into eighths lengthwise.   Dry between towels and fry in deep fat.   Drain on soft paper, sprinkle with salt and serve in an uncovered dish.   The fat must not be too hot, as the potatoes must be cooked as well as browned.

POTATO DROPS

2 cups mashed potatoes (without any milk)	2 eggs Salt and pepper

Mix the potato and the beaten eggs.   Drop the mixture from a spoon into the hot fat and fry until a golden brown, then drain on brown paper and serve with a garnish of parsley.   If the spoon is dipped in boiling water after every using, each drop will retain the shape of the spoon.

POTATO O'BRIEN

6 medium-sized potatoes Salt	Chopped pimientos Onion-juice

Wash, pare and cut potatoes into half-inch dice.   Dry between towels.   Fry in hot fat until a delicate brown.   Drain on soft paper, sprinkle with salt, then sauté them in just enough fat to keep them from burning, adding finely chopped pimientos and a few drops of onion-juice.   These should be tossed frequently during cooking, and not pressed close to the pan.

POTATOES ON THE HALF-SHELL

Select medium-sized potatoes and bake.   Remove the top of each potato so as to make it boat shape.   Scoop out the inside, being careful not to break the shell.   Mash very thoroughly— it is well to put them through a ricer—add butter, salt and hot milk and beat well.   Pile the mixture lightly into the shells, do not smooth down the top, stand each in a shallow pan, return to the oven and brown lightly on top.   A quick oven is required to brown the potatoes.

If the potatoes are too large for a single serving, they may be cut in two lengthwise, and each half may be stuffed.

STUFFED POTATO

Follow directions for potatoes on the half-shell, adding one-half cup peanut butter and two egg-whites to the potato mixture.

POTATOES SUZETTE

6 medium-sized potatoes
½ cup hot milk
2 tablespoons melted butter
6 eggs
6 tablespoons buttered crums
1 tablespoon grated cheese
Salt and pepper

Prepare as for stuffed potatoes. Refill the shell almost to the top, break an egg into each opening, season with pepper and salt and sprinkle with buttered crums that have been mixed with grated cheese and bake long enough to set the eggs as well as for poached eggs. Brown lightly (about six minutes).

DELMONICO POTATOES

2 cups cooked potatoes, diced
2 cups medium white sauce
Salt and pepper
Buttered crums

Mix potatoes and sauce, pour into a buttered baking-dish, cover with crums and bake fifteen minutes in a hot oven.

HASHED BROWN POTATOES

2 tablespoons oil or drippings
6 boiled potatoes
Salt and pepper

Chop the potatoes, adding salt, and a dash of pepper. Melt the fat in a frying-pan and, when hot, add the chopped potatoes to the depth of one inch. Press the potatoes down in the pan, packing them firmly. Cook slowly, without stirring, until the potato is brown. Then begin at one side of the pan and fold the potatoes over on the other like an omelet, packing closely together. Turn upside down on a hot serving platter and serve hot.

LYONNAISE POTATOES

2 cups boiled potatoes, diced
1 tablespoon minced onion
2 tablespoons drippings
1 tablespoon chopped parsley

The potatoes should be rather underdone to produce the best results. Season with salt and pepper. Cook the onion in fat until yellow, add the diced potato and stir with a fork until all sides are brown, being careful not to break the potatoes. Add more fat if necessary. When done, turn the potatoes out upon a hot dish, sprinkle parsley over the top, and serve hot.

SPANISH POTATOES

1 tablespoon minced onion
2 tablespoons chopped green pepper
2 tablespoons chopped pimiento
4 tablespoons oil or drippings

2 cups cold boiled potatoes, diced
½ cup cold cooked ham, chopped
1 teaspoon salt
½ teaspoon paprika

Fry the onion, pepper and pimiento in the fat until light brown, add the diced potatoes, the chopped ham and seasonings and cook until thoroughly heated through.

GLAZED SWEET POTATOES

6 sweet potatoes
Salt and pepper
Butter

1 cup brown sugar
¼ cup water

Boil the potatoes without paring them, and, when tender, drain and strip off the skins. Make a thick sirup of the sugar and water. Cut each potato in half, dip it in the sirup, lay in a baking-dish, season each piece with salt and pepper, a bit of butter. Bake in a quick oven until the potatoes are brown. They will brown quickly.

SWEET-POTATO PUFF

2 cups mashed sweet potato
2 tablespoons butter
Salt and pepper

¼ cup milk or cream
1 egg

To the mashed potatoes add the melted fat, seasonings and milk. Beat the egg-yolk and white separately, add the yolk to the potato mixture and then fold in the white. Bake in one dish or in individual molds until puffy and brown.

SWEET POTATO WITH PINEAPPLE

6 small sweet potatoes   ⅓ cup honey
⅓ as much pineapple as potato   ¼ cup water

Boil the potatoes with the skins on. When cool, peel and cut
them in pieces one-quarter of an inch thick. Mix honey and hot
water. Just cover the bottom of a baking-dish with the mixture,
add a layer of sweet potatoes with sliced pineapple. Pour the
remaining honey mixture over them and bake for ten minutes in
the oven.

MASHED SWEET-POTATO CARAMEL

2 cups mashed sweet potato   ½ cup maple sirup
Milk   ¼ cup butter
Pepper and salt

Left-over sweet potatoes, either baked or boiled, may be used
for this dish. Mash potatoes and add sufficient milk or cream to
make a smooth, soft paste. Season with pepper and salt. Put in
well-greased casserole or baking-dish, suitable for serving at table,
and pour in thick maple sirup which has been boiled with butter.
Bake until the top begins to caramelize.

CREAMED SALSIFY OR OYSTER PLANT

Wash and scrape the salsify, throwing it immediately into cold
water to which a little vinegar or lemon-juice has been added, to
prevent discoloration. Cut in inch slices and cook in boiling
water until tender, adding salt just before cooking is completed.
When tender, drain and combine with medium white sauce. Serve
with tiny fried sausage balls.

BOILED SPINACH

2 pounds spinach   3 tablespoons butter
Salt and pepper

Remove roots and wilted leaves of the spinach. Wash in several
waters, until all trace of sand has disappeared. Place in a large
kettle without additional water; the water which clings to the
leaves is sufficient. Cover the kettle and cook until the spinach
is tender. The time of cooking depends on the age of the spinach.
Long cooking darkens it. Salt the water just before cooking is
completed. When done, drain, chop, season with salt, pepper and

butter. One tablespoon lemon-juice may be added while chopping, if desired. Garnish with slices of hard-cooked eggs if desired.

SUCCOTASH

2 cups green corn or 1 cup
  dried corn
2 cups fresh Lima, string or
  butter beans or 1 cup dried
  Lima beans

Salt and pepper
1 cup milk
4 tablespoons **butter**

If fresh vegetables are used, cut the **corn from the cob. Cover** the beans with the least possible amount of boiling water, to prevent scorching, and cook until tender. Drain off the water, add the corn and the milk and cook slowly until the corn is tender. Add the butter and other seasoning.

When dried corn and beans are used, soak both separately overnight. In the morning, cover the beans with fresh water, and boil them very gently until tender. Do not drain the water from the corn, but set the pan containing it on the back of the range where it will cook slowly. When the beans are tender, drain and add them to the corn, allowing only water enough to cover them. Cook slowly until tender and drain off water and save for soup. Add the milk and seasoning.

BAKED TOMATOES

6 tomatoes
4 tablespoons **butter**
Salt and pepper

1 cup bread-crums
1 teaspoon sugar

Peel the tomatoes and cut them in slices one-fourth of an inch thick. Place a layer of tomatoes in a pudding-dish, and sprinkle over them a little salt and pepper. Rub the butter into the crums with the sugar. Spread the mixture thickly upon the tomatoes, using all of it, and add another layer of tomatoes. Add bits of butter, sprinkle with dry crums, and bake twenty minutes.

BROILED TOMATOES

6 tomatoes
Salt and pepper

Melted butter

Choose firm, round tomatoes, cut them into slices, three-quarters inch thick, dust each slice with salt and pepper, place in a greased

broiler and broil over a moderate fire until tender. Turn once
carefully. Add melted butter when sending to the table.

STUFFED TOMATOES

6 tomatoes

1½ cups soft bread-crums

¼ teaspoon pepper

2 tablespoons butter or savory
fat

1 teaspoon salt

The tomatoes should be very firm, smooth, and of equal size.
Cut a piece from the stem end of each tomato, and remove the
centers without breaking the walls. Make a stuffing of the centers
of the tomatoes, crums, seasonings, and melted butter or savory
fat, and mix well. Sprinkle each tomato well with salt and pepper and fill with the stuffing, packing it in quite solidly.

Place a small piece of butter or fat on the top of each, arrange
the tomatoes in a baking-dish and bake in a moderate oven until
tender. Serve hot in the baking-dish.

TURNIPS IN CREAM

8 turnips

2 cups milk

4 tablespoons flour

4 tablespoons butter or other
fat

Salt and pepper

Pare the turnips, cut them in small pieces, cook until tender.
Make a white sauce of the flour, fat, milk and seasonings. Pour
sauce over turnips and serve.

SALADS AND SALAD DRESSINGS

CARDINAL SALAD

2 large beets
2 tablespoons vinegar
½ cup wax beans
½ cup peas
½ cup asparagus tips

Mayonnaise made with vinegar
  from beets
Lettuce
Radishes for a garnish

Boil beets until tender, slice, cover with vinegar and let stand until the following day. Drain off the vinegar and use it in making the mayonnaise. Arrange white wax beans, peas, asparagus tips and red mayonnaise in little rose-like nests of lettuce leaves, and garnish with red radishes.

CABBAGE SALAD

½ head cabbage
6 eggs
½ cup sugar
1 teaspoon salt

1 teaspoon mustard
2 teaspoons melted butter
¼ cup vinegar

Cut the cabbage in several parts, and wash it well. Remove wilted or tough leaves, cut out the core and chop very fine with a sharp knife. Cook the eggs hard, chop five of them very fine, place the cabbage in a salad-bowl, add the chopped eggs, and toss and fold lightly together. Mix the sugar, salt, mustard and vinegar well together and pour this liquid over the cabbage and eggs. Toss again lightly with a fork held in each hand, arrange in a dish, and garnish with the remaining egg cut in slices.

COLE-SLAW

¼ cup vinegar
1½ teaspoon salt
¼ teaspoon pepper
1 tablespoon sugar

3 eggs
1 tablespoon butter
2 tablespoons cream
3 cups cabbage

Heat vinegar and seasonings (including the sugar and butter) to boiling, beat eggs and add hot vinegar mixture to them very slowly. Cook in double boiler until the mixture thickens and then add cream. Remove the dressing from the fire and pour it while hot over the cabbage. Garnish with rings of hard-cooked eggs and serve when cold.

CARROT SALAD

1 cup grated raw carrot
1 cup chopped raw cabbage or celery, or cabbage and celery combined

1 tablespoon lemon-juice
½ teaspoon salt
Mayonnaise or boiled dressing
Lettuce leaves

Mix the ingredients well and serve on crisp lettuce leaves. The grated carrot may be combined also with cold boiled peas, with chopped nuts and apples, or with onions and radishes.

CUCUMBER JELLY SALAD

1 pint grated cucumber
Salt and paprika
2 tablespoons vinegar
1 tablespoon oil
1 tablespoon gelatin

2 teaspoons cold water
6 halves of walnut-meats
Mayonnaise
Lettuce leaves

Peel cucumbers, removing most of the white as well as the green skin. Grate enough to give one pint and season with salt, paprika, vinegar and oil. Add gelatin mixed with cold water. Place over the fire until warm and well mixed, not boiled. In the bottom of individual molds put a half kernel of walnut, then pour in the cucumber mixture and set on the ice to cool. When ready to serve, turn each mold on to a nest of young lettuce leaves, and add a spoonful of mayonnaise.

LETTUCE SALAD

Choose for this the crisp center of the lettuce. Wash it, dry it well, pull to pieces or cut it into four or six sections, and arrange it in a salad-bowl. Pour over the center of the dish any dressing preferred. Mayonnaise is frequently used, but with a heavy dinner the French dressing is to be preferred to any other. Russian dressing is very much used.

The following vegetables may be used instead of lettuce: endive, peppergrass, watercress, nasturtium blossoms, sorrel, dandelion, escarole, and romaine.

POTATO SALAD

1 quart new potatoes
1 tablespoon oil
2 tablespoons vinegar
1 onion
2 stalks celery
Lemon
1 tablespoon capers

1 tablespoon chopped parsley
Salt and pepper
Thin mayonnaise or boiled
   dressing
Cut beets
Lettuce

Boil potatoes until done, but not too soft, slice them when cooked and add oil and vinegar. Chop onion and celery very fine, and add, with capers, parsley, and salt and pepper to taste. Pour a thin mayonnaise over the potatoes, mixing thoroughly with a wooden spoon. Garnish with lettuce, a few pieces of lemon and cut beets.

TOMATO AND CELERY SALAD

6 tomatoes
2 cups celery, diced

⅓ to ½ cup mayonnaise
Lettuce leaves

Select firm tomatoes of a good size, cut a slice from the top of each, and scoop out all the seeds and soft pulp, being careful not to break the sides. Cut celery into small dice, mix it with mayonnaise dressing, fill the shells with the mixture, place one teaspoon of the dressing on top of each tomato and serve individually on a bed of lettuce leaves, placing three or four small leaves on each plate and the tomato in the center.

TOMATO SURPRISE SALAD

6 tomatoes
¾ cup diced cucumber
½ cup diced, cooked chicken
¼ cup chopped nuts

¼ cup mayonnaise dressing
Lettuce
Garnish of truffles or walnut-
   meats

Select medium-sized, smooth tomatoes. Scald and remove the skins. Chill. Carefully scoop the inside out of the tomatoes. Remove the seeds from the pulp. Chill all ingredients, and when ready to serve, mix the chicken, cucumber, tomato pulp, and nuts with the mayonnaise dressing. Add more salt if needed. Fill the tomatoes.

Arrange on lettuce leaves. Garnish with mayonnaise and

decorate each tomato top with a slice of truffle or with halves or shelled nuts.

FROZEN FRUIT SALAD

1 pint cream
1½ cups fruit cut fine (cherries, peaches, pineapple, etc.)
¾ cup mayonnaise
1 teaspoon powdered sugar

1 teaspoon instantaneous gelatin
2 tablespoons cold water
Lettuce

Soak the gelatin in the cold water, melt it over steam, and beat it into the mayonnaise. Add the sugar to the cream and whip it, then combine with the mayonnaise. Stir in the cut-up fruit. Pack in ice and freeze as for a mousse. The mayonnaise may be omitted from the mixture to be frozen and served separately.

TOMATO JELLY SALAD

2 cups canned tomato juice
1 slice onion
1 stalk celery
1 bay-leaf
1 clove
¼ green pepper pod

1 teaspoon sugar
Salt
2 tablespoons gelatin
½ cup cold water
Lettuce
Mayonnaise

Cook tomato juice with seasonings. Soak gelatin and add to tomato juice, strain and pour into cups about the size of a tomato. Make a nest of small green lettuce leaves for each mold when serving, and place one tablespoon of mayonnaise on top of each tomato as it is turned from the mold.

Tomato jelly is often molded in a square pan and cut in diamonds or cubes, when it makes a very acceptable accessory to other salads and an attractive garnish.

ALLIGATOR-PEAR SALAD

2 alligator pears
Lettuce leaves

½ to ¾ cup mayonnaise or French dressing

Alligator pears, or avocadoes, are to be had at fancy fruiterers. Cut each pear into six pieces, giving wedge-shaped sections, and if these are too large, cut each section again lengthwise. Peel and arrange wedges of pears on beds of lettuce leaves. Serve with

French dressing to which has been added cut orange pulp and
a few preserved sweet onions. Some prefer the pear with simple
lemon dressing.

BANANA AND NUT SALAD

3 bananas
½ cup nuts
6 leaves lettuce

½ cup mayonnaise or boiled
dressing

Peel bananas and cut in two lengthwise. Roll in nut-meats.
Place on lettuce leaf and garnish with dressing. Equal parts of
dressing and whipped cream may be used.

COCONUT FRUIT SALAD

1½ cups mixed diced tart apples and celery
½ cup shredded coconut
1 tablespoon lemon-juice
4 tablespoons oil

4 tablespoons orange-juice
Salt
Paprika
Lettuce leaves
Currant or plum jelly

Mix the apples, celery, and coconut. Sprinkle with the lemon-
juice. Add a French dressing made from the oil and orange-juice,
with salt and paprika to taste. Line a salad-bowl with lettuce
leaves and pile chilled salad in center. Dot with currant or plum
jelly.

COMBINATION FRUIT SALAD

6 halves of stewed pears, fresh
or canned
Lettuce leaves

36 white cherries
Boiled dressing

Place the half pears on crisp lettuce leaves. Stone the cherries
and arrange them around the pears. Serve with a boiled
dressing.

FRENCH FRUIT SALAD

1 orange
1 banana
½ pound Malaga grapes

1 dozen English walnuts
Lettuce
French dressing

Peel the oranges and cut away the sections from the membrane
by placing a knife parallel with the membrane and slicing down.
If the fruit is allowed to stand in cold water after peeling, the
bitter white membrane will come off easily.

Peel the bananas and cut in quarter-inch slices. Remove the skins and seeds from the grapes. Break in small pieces, but do not chop, the walnut-meats. Mix these ingredients thoroughly and place on ice. When ready to serve, place on lettuce leaves and serve with French dressing. This salad is pretty served in an orange basket, or, by substituting the grapefruit pulp for the orange, it may be properly served in the shell of a half grapefruit.

GRAPEFRUIT AND GRAPE SALAD

2 cups grapefruit sections
2 tablespoons grape-juice
2 tablespoons French dressing
½ cup Malaga grapes, peeled and seeded

Peel fine large grapefruit and separate the sections, removing every particle of the bitter white inner skin. Peel and seed the grapes and mix with the grapefruit. Set aside, covered, on ice until very cold. Pour over them the grape-juice and French dressing.

PEAR SALAD

6 pears
6 stalks celery
Mayonnaise
Salt and pepper
½ cup broken walnut-meats and stoned olives, chopped
Lettuce leaves

Select well-formed pears and cut off a bit of the broad end so that the pear will stand steadily on the plate. With a potato-ball cutter remove the center, leaving enough of the pear to make a thick cup. Cut the celery into dice, add broken walnut-meats and chopped olives and mix all together with mayonnaise, adding a pinch of salt and pepper. Fill the pear cups and serve on lettuce leaves.

PINEAPPLE AND CREAM-CHEESE SALAD

6 slices canned pineapple
1 cup cream cheese
Purple grape-juice
French dressing
Lettuce leaves

Work enough grape-juice into the cream cheese to soften it so that it can be made into balls with the hands or with butter paddles. Add the grape-juice cautiously so as not to make the mixture too soft to handle. Place a slice of pineapple on a lettuce leaf, put a cheese ball on top and pour grape-juice and French dressing over all.

TROPICAL SALAD

1 cup cantaloup balls
6 slices tomato
Garnish of red pepper

Any desired dressing
Lettuce leaves

With a vegetable cutter, cut small balls from a cantaloup that is fairly firm in texture. Arrange several balls on a slice of tomato which has been placed on a nest of lettuce leaves. Garnish with pieces of red pepper or green pepper cut in diamond shapes. Serve with any desired dressing.

SALAD EGGS

6 hard-cooked eggs
1 tablespoon butter
1 tablespoon cream
½ teaspoon mustard
Pinch cayenne

1 teaspoon salt
1 tablespoon anchovy paste
Lettuce or cress
Garnish of radishes and small
onions

Remove the shells from the cold, hard-cooked eggs and cut a large piece from the top of each, take out the yolks and mix them to form a paste with butter, cream, mustard, cayenne, salt and anchovy paste. Put this mixture back into the hollows and lay the eggs on a dish of lettuce or cress. Garnish with radishes and small onions.

CHICKEN SALAD

2 cups diced chicken
1 cup diced celery
Mayonnaise
Lettuce

Garnish of celery tops, beets
cut into dice, capers, egg-
yolks, etc.

Left-over chicken makes a very good salad. To prepare a chicken especially for salad, rub well with salt and pepper, place one small onion and one bay-leaf inside, wrap with a napkin, tie securely and steam for three hours, or until a fork can be easily turned around in the meat. When the chicken is cold, cut the breast with a knife into pieces not too small and sprinkle with French dressing. The dark meat should not be used if a pretty salad is desired. If dark meat is used, cut in smaller cubes than white meat and the white meat will predominate in appearance. Marinate the chicken mixture and let it stand. Make a mayonnaise dressing, stir part of it into the celery, place the latter on a thin layer of lettuce, or else arrange it directly upon the salad-dish and dispose the tips of the celery prettily about the edge. Heap the chicken mixture in the center, pour over it the remainder of the mayonnaise, and garnish with white celery tops, beets cut in dice, capers, cold hard-boiled yolks of eggs that have been pressed through a colander, or any other arrangement that pleases the fancy.

FISH SALAD

1 pound haddock or other fish	1 cup chopped celery
2 tablespoons oil	Lettuce
1 tablespoon vinegar	Mayonnaise

Wrap the haddock in a clean cloth and boil it for ten minutes in salted water. The remains of almost any cold fish may be used in this way very satisfactorily, but the salad is more successful when made of fish that will flake nicely, such as salmon, cod, haddock, or halibut. Canned salmon will also make a very good salad. Remove the bones, pick the fish into fine bits while hot, turn over it oil mixed with vinegar and set away in a cold place. When about to serve, chop celery and add to the fish. Arrange crisp white leaves of lettuce in cup shapes on a platter, using one or two leaves for each, then lay one spoonful of the mixture in each cup and pour over it one spoonful of mayonnaise.

LOBSTER SALAD

1½ cups diced lobster meat	Mayonnaise
½ cup diced celery	Lettuce
Vinegar	

Remove the meat from fresh boiled lobster chilled. Reserve the creamy or green fat, together with the coral. If there are eggs on the tail fins, save them also. Cut the meat not too small. Sprinkle a very little vinegar over the lobster, but keep the celery crisp until it is time to make the salad. Then mix the meat and celery together, stir in enough mayonnaise to moisten and flavor the whole. Arrange the salad on the center of a bed of crisp white lettuce bordered with green lettuce leaves laid under the outer edges. Pour on the remainder of the mayonnaise and sprinkle over it the coral, well pounded, and if liked the eggs and a few capers. Garnish with the claws. Sometimes lettuce leaves are arranged on a platter in cup-like clusters of two or three each, and the salad is divided equally among the clusters. The salad may be served in the cleaned lobster shells.

SARDINE SALAD

¾ cup sardines   Lettuce leaves
¾ cup hard-cooked egg   Mayonnaise or French dressing
1 cucumber

Remove the skin and bones from sardines and mix with chopped hard-cooked eggs. Cut cucumber in thin slices and arrange on lettuce leaves. Add sardine and egg mixture. Serve with mayonnaise or French dressing.

SHRIMP SALAD

1 pint cooked shrimps or   Lettuce, shredded celery, or
  prawns, fresh or canned   shaved cabbage
Marinade   Mayonnaise or other dressing

Marinate the shrimps and serve whole on lettuce, shredded celery, or finely shaved cabbage, and cover well with a mayonnaise or other dressing. Canned shrimps are excellent for salads.

MISCELLANEOUS COMBINATIONS FOR SALADS

1. Asparagus and tomato
2. Cabbage, pineapple and coconut
3. Pea, cheese and pickle
4. Mashed potatoes, combined with pimiento, green pepper and hard-cooked egg
5. Pineapple, marshmallow and nuts
6. Rice and carrots
7. Molded fruit gelatin
8. Orange, prune and nut
9. Prunes stuffed with cottage-cheese
10. Carrot and shredded lettuce
11. Beet and cabbage salad
12. Beet and egg salad
13. Cabbage, celery and watercress
14. Mixed vegetables
15. Orange and Bermuda onion
16. Tomato, cucumber, onion

FRENCH DRESSING

3 tablespoons oil	$\frac{3}{4}$ teaspoon pepper
$\frac{3}{4}$ to 1 tablespoon vinegar or lemon-juice	1 teaspoon salt

These ingredients make a simple French dressing. Many salad-lovers add one or more other ingredients to give a particular tang or flavor. The French always rub the bowl in which the salad-dressing is made with a clove of garlic. Tarragon, or estragon, vinegar may be used instead of plain vinegar, or some leaves of tarragon or estragon, procurable at the large markets, may be cut in bits and sprinkled over the salad.

If the French dressing is made at table, a small china or glass tray, set with oil and vinegar cruets, salt-cellar, peppercorn-grinder, paprika-shaker, bottle of Worcestershire sauce, and a bottle of pearl onions, is passed to the person who serves the salad. Small silver stands for holding these ingredients are now found in the shops.

Mix the oil, salt and pepper together and slowly add the vinegar, stirring constantly. In dressing a salad at the table, the dressing may be made in a separate bowl and then poured upon the vegetables, the latter being tossed lightly for a few seconds and then served, or it may be done in the following graceful way: Hold a salad-spoon (or a tablespoon) over the salad, put into it the salt and the pepper, and then fill with the oil the remaining space, mix with a fork, and then pour upon the vegetables, distributing well; add the remaining proportion of oil, a spoonful at a time, tossing the salad lightly; at the last add the vinegar, toss again and serve. Or all ingredients may be placed in a cruet and shaken vigorously, then poured over the salad.

If the French dressing is made before the meal, the addition of a small amount of egg-white beaten with the dressing will make the emulsion more permanent.

VARIATIONS FOR FRENCH DRESSING

Many variations may be made by the addition of other ingredients to the French dressing. Grated cheese may be added, also bits of parsley, catchup, horseradish, garlic, green peppers, and other condiments.

MAYONNAISE DRESSING

All materials should be thoroughly chilled before being used in the making of mayonnaise.

2 raw egg-yolks
½ teaspoon salt
¼ teaspoon pepper
¼ teaspoon paprika

⅛ teaspoon mustard
3 tablespoons vinegar or lemon-juice
2 cups olive oil or substitute

To the yolks add the seasonings, beat thoroughly, add the vinegar, or lemon-juice, and beat again. Add the oil gradually (drop by drop at first). The mixture should be thick and creamy. Should the mayonnaise curdle, begin with a third egg-yolk, add a small quantity of oil to the egg, and then by very small quantities, add the curdled dressing. At times a dressing may be quite firm when left, only to be found curdled and disappointing when the time comes to use it. This third-egg process will, however, usually restore it. Equal proportions of vinegar and lemon-juice may be used. Tarragon vinegar is sometimes used instead of the ordinary kind.

VARIATIONS IN THE MAKING OF MAYONNAISE DRESSING

Mayonnaise dressing takes on a new flavor if chopped pickles, olives, mangoes, pimiento or celery are added.

Mayonnaise may be extended by adding a corn-starch paste to it. This paste may be made on the proportion of two tablespoons of corn-starch to one cup of water. It must be smooth, transparent and well-cooked, so that the corn-starch taste is destroyed. If this paste is used, the mayonnaise needs to be seasoned more highly.

COLORED MAYONNAISE

Mayonnaise may be colored green in the following manner: Boil two cups of spinach until tender, drain it, let it cool and squeeze dry. Mash it thoroughly by pounding, adding one spoonful of the mayonnaise, pass the whole through a fine sieve and mix with the dressing. A lighter shade may be obtained by boiling and mashing green peas and using them in the same way.

To produce a red tint for a lobster or fish salad, pound the coral of a lobster, pass it through a fine sieve, and add it to the dressing.

THOUSAND ISLAND SALAD DRESSING

1 cup mayonnaise
4 tablespoons chilli sauce
1 tablespoon chives
3 tablespoons catchup
1 teaspoon tarragon vinegar

1 tablespoon chopped green pepper
3 tablespoons chopped red pepper
1 teaspoon paprika

Add chilli sauce, chives, catchup, peppers, paprika and vinegar to mayonnaise.

BOILED DRESSING

1/4 cup vinegar
3/4 tablespoon sugar
1/4 tablespoon flour
1/8 tablespoon mustard

1/4 teaspoon salt
1/8 teaspoon pepper
1 egg-yolk
1/4 tablespoon butter

Heat the vinegar. Sift the dry ingredients thoroughly, add to the slightly beaten egg-yolk, and beat together well. Pour the boiling vinegar gradually upon the mixture, stirring constantly. Put in the upper part of the double boiler and cook over hot water until it thickens, stirring all the time. Add the butter and remove from the fire. Serve when cold, with or without the addition of cream, which may be whipped.

This kind of dressing may also be bought on the market. When made at home, the beaten whites of eggs or cream, plain or whipped, are often added before serving.

SOUR-CREAM SALAD DRESSING

1 teaspoon salt
1 teaspoon sugar
1/8 teaspoon cayenne

1 tablespoon lemon-juice
2 tablespoons vinegar
1 cup sour cream

This makes an excellent dressing for vegetable salads. Place the salt, sugar, and pepper together in a bowl, mix well and add the lemon-juice, then the vinegar. When the mixture is perfectly smooth, put in the cream, stir well and set on the ice until needed.

DRESSING FOR MEAT SALADS

Tartar sauce and Hollandaise sauce can be used with meat salads very nicely, if desired.

COOKIES AND SMALL CAKES

PLAIN COOKIES

⅓ cup butter or shortening
½ cup sugar
1 egg
2 teaspoons baking-powder

2 cups flour
⅛ teaspoon salt
½ cup milk
½ teaspoon vanilla

Cream together thoroughly the butter or shortening and the sugar. Add the slightly beaten egg. Mix and sift the dry ingredients and add alternately with the milk to the first mixture. Add flavoring. Toss on lightly floured board, roll thin, cut and place on a greased baking-sheet. Bake in a moderate oven (350° F.) twelve to fifteen minutes.

LEMON WAFERS

1 cup butter or shortening
2 cups sugar

3 eggs
3 tablespoons lemon-juice
Flour

Cream the butter or shortening, add the sugar and well-beaten eggs, and lemon-juice. Stir in flour enough to make as soft a dough as can be rolled. Roll very thin and shape with a cutter. Bake at 380° F. for 10 min. This recipe may be used for vanilla, chocolate, or orange wafers.

CARAWAY COOKIES

½ cup butter or shortening
1 cup sugar
1 egg
2 cups flour

2 teaspoons baking-powder
½ teaspoon salt
¾ cup milk
1½ tablespoons caraway seeds

Cream the butter or shortening with the sugar; add beaten egg. Mix and sift the flour, baking-powder, and salt, and add alternately with the milk to the first mixture. Add caraway seeds.

126

Toss on lightly floured board.   Roll out about one-half inch
thick and cut in fancy shapes.   Place on greased baking-sheet
and bake in moderate oven (380-390° F.) twelve to fifteen
minutes.

"FROZEN" COOKIES

2 cups melted shortening	1 teaspoon cinnamon
1 cup white sugar	4 cups flour
1 cup brown sugar	1 teaspoon soda
3 eggs	Brazil nuts, filberts or almonds
1 teaspoon salt	

Mix ingredients in the order given, sifting all the dry ingredients
together before adding.   Mold in long rolls or pack in a deep
pan like a bread-pan and roll in clean cloth.   Let stand in a cold
place until hard.   Slice thin, and bake in a moderate oven (380-
390° F.) until a golden brown.   A roll may be kept indefinitely
in a cold place.

These cookies are excellent to keep on hand, especially when
the dough can be kept out-of-doors in cold weather.   In case of an
emergency they are easily brought in and quickly baked.   Nuts
in these cookies are very attractive when put in whole.

FILLED COOKIES

1 cup sugar	3½ cups flour
½ cup shortening	3 teaspoons baking-powder
1 egg	½ teaspoon salt
½ cup milk	1 teaspoon vanilla

Mix ingredients in order given, sifting the flour with the baking-
powder and salt before adding it.   Roll thin, cut, and put in
greased pans.   Place a teaspoon of filling on each, not allowing it
to spread to the edge, place another cookie on top, press down the
edges, and bake in shallow pans in a moderate oven (380-390°
F.).

For the filling, take:

½ cup sugar	1 cup chopped raisins
1 tablespoon flour	½ cup water

Mix sugar and flour together, add to the other ingredients, and
cook until thick, stirring constantly.   Dates, figs, prunes, apricots,
or any marmalade may be used instead of raisins.

BROWN-SUGAR COOKIES

2 cups brown sugar
1 cup melted shortening
3 eggs
¼ cup milk

1 tablespoon vanilla
1 teaspoon soda
Flour to mix stiff

Mix ingredients in order given. Add just enough flour to roll.
Cut into shapes as desired. Sprinkle with brown sugar, and bake
in a moderate oven (380° F.).

CHOCOLATE DROP COOKIES

2 squares chocolate
½ cup butter or shortening
1 cup brown sugar
½ teaspoon soda

1 egg
2 cups flour
¾ cup sweet milk

Melt the chocolate and add to the melted shortening. Add sugar,
egg, milk, and soda and flour sifted together. Batter should be
stiff enough to drop from the spoon. Drop by spoonfuls on
greased pans, and bake in a moderate oven (350-375° F.). Frost,
if desired.

BROWNIES

2 squares chocolate
¼ cup fat
1 cup white sugar
1 egg

½ teaspoon salt
½ cup flour
½ cup nuts

Melt chocolate and add it to the melted fat. Add sugar, egg, salt
and flour. Mix in chopped nuts, pour in greased baking-pans,
and bake at 360° F. about twenty-five minutes. They will look
half baked, but mark off in squares or strips when you take them
from the oven, and they will harden as they cool. Remove from
the pans when cool. Serve with afternoon tea. These cookies
resemble fudge in taste and appearance.

GINGER SNAPS

1 cup molasses
½ cup butter or shortening
1 teaspoon salt

3 cups flour
1 teaspoon soda
2 teaspoons ginger

Heat the molasses and shortening. Mix and sift the dry ingredients and add to first mixture. Thoroughly chill, toss on

lightly floured board, and roll out very thin. Cut as desired. The bowl containing the remaining dough must be kept in a cool place or it will be necessary to add more flour. Excess flour will make the cookies hard and unattractive. Put on greased baking-sheet and bake in a moderate oven (320-390° F.) twelve to fifteen minutes.

PEANUT COOKIES

¼ cup butter or shortening	½ teaspoon salt
1 cup brown sugar	2 cups flour
2 eggs	2 teaspoons baking-powder
¼ cup milk	1 to 2 cups chopped peanuts

Melt fat, add brown sugar, eggs and milk. Add sifted salt, flour and baking-powder, and chopped peanuts. Drop by teaspoonfuls on greased pans, an inch or two apart. Place a half peanut on each and bake in a quick oven (400° F.).

RAISIN ROCKS

1 cup butter or shortening	1 teaspoon ginger
1 cup brown sugar	2 teaspoons soda
1 teaspoon salt	2 cups molasses
Flour	1 cup seeded raisins

Cook the butter or shortening, sugar, molasses, ginger and salt together. Stir the mixture until it boils and boil it five minutes. Pour into a bowl and stir in flour and soda sifted together until it is stiff enough to drop from a spoon. Add the raisins and drop from a spoon on to a greased shallow pan. Bake the rocks in a moderate oven (380° F.).

HERMITS

½ cup butter or shortening	1 teaspoon each of all kinds of
½ cup sugar	spice
2 eggs	½ teaspoon soda
1 cup chopped raisins	Flour
1 tablespoon molasses	

Cream fat, add sugar gradually. Add eggs, molasses and raisins. Sift soda and spices with one cup of flour, and mix all thoroughly. Add enough flour to make quite a stiff dough, and roll. Bake in a moderate oven (380° F.).

OATMEAL COOKIES

½ cup sugar
½ cup molasses
¾ cup fat
2 eggs
¼ cup sweet milk
2 teaspoons cinnamon

1 teaspoon cloves
1 teaspoon soda
2 cups flour
1 cup chopped raisins
2 cups oatmeal

Mix ingredients in the order given. Melt the fat before adding it, and sift the soda and spices with the flour. Drop by teaspoonfuls on greased pans and bake in a moderate oven (380° F.).

BOHEMIAN CHRISTMAS COOKIES

Yolks of 2 hard-cooked eggs
⅓ cup butter or shortening
⅓ cup sugar
Yolk of 1 egg

1 tablespoon milk
Flour to stiffen for rolling
3 tablespoons finely chopped blanched almonds

Put the hard-cooked yolks of eggs through a ricer or sieve and cream with the butter or shortening. Add the sugar, cream again, then stir in the uncooked egg-yolk, the milk, and sifted flour. The dough should be stiff enough to roll. Cut into small round shapes with cooky-cutters, brush these with beaten egg-white and sprinkle with finely chopped almonds. Bake in a slow oven (300° F.).

CHRISTMAS PEPPERNUTS

2 cups brown sugar
2 eggs
1 teaspoon soda
1 tablespoon hot water

1 cup chopped nuts
2 teaspoons cinnamon
1 teaspoon nutmeg
3½ cups sifted bread flour

Mix the sugar with the well-beaten eggs, add the soda dissolved in hot water, the nuts, and the spices sifted with the flour. Add more flour if necessary to make a dough stiff enough to roll. Roll out until the dough is about one-eighth inch thick. Cut in tiny rounds about as large as a quarter of a dollar and bake in a quick oven (400° F.) until brown. Roll at once in powdered sugar.

SWEET-MILK DOUGHNUTS

1 tablespoon butter or fat	3 teaspoons baking-powder
1 cup sugar	1 teaspoon salt
2 eggs	1 teaspoon nutmeg
1 cup milk	Flour

Beat the eggs till very light, add the sugar and when foamy add the melted butter or fat. Sift the baking-powder, salt and nutmeg with one cup of flour and stir into first mixture, alternating with the milk so as to keep the mixture smooth. Add just enough flour to make a soft dough which can be handled. Roll out three-fourths inch thick on a lightly floured board. A soft dough makes light, tender doughnuts when cooked. Fry in deep fat and drain on unglazed paper. Test the fat for temperature or by using a thermometer. Fat should never smoke, as this produces harmful by-products.

Roll the doughnuts in powdered sugar just before serving.

SOUR-MILK DOUGHNUTS

1 cup sugar	1/2 teaspoon salt
1 tablespoon sour cream	1/2 teaspoon cinnamon
2 eggs	1/2 teaspoon nutmeg
1 cup sour milk	Flour
1/2 teaspoon soda	

Mix the sugar with the cream and add the beaten eggs and sour milk. Sift the soda, salt and spices with one cup of flour and add to the first mixture. Add additional flour to make a dough just stiff enough to handle. Toss on a floured board, roll out, and cut. Fry in deep fat. Test temperature of fat as in sweet-milk doughnuts. Drain on unglazed paper. When cold, roll in powdered sugar.

CRULLERS

1/4 cup butter or shortening	3 1/2 teaspoons baking-powder
1 cup sugar	1/4 teaspoon grated nutmeg
2 eggs	1/2 teaspoon salt
1 cup milk	Flour

Cream the butter or shortening. Add sugar; then the well-beaten eggs. Sift the baking-powder, nutmeg, and salt with one cup of flour and add alternately with the milk to the first mixture. Add additional flour to make a dough stiff enough to handle. Toss on floured board, roll one-half inch thick and cut into strips. Twist and fry in deep fat. Test temperature of fat as in sweet-milk doughnuts. Drain on unglazed paper and when cold roll in powdered sugar. This recipe makes about three dozen crullers.

GINGERBREAD

½ cup molasses	½ teaspoon soda
½ cup sugar	1 cup flour
½ cup melted fat	1 teaspoon ginger
½ cup sour milk	2 teaspoons cinnamon
1 egg	Nutmeg

Mix ingredients in order given, sifting the soda with the flour before adding it. Bake in a slow oven in a greased shallow pan or in muffin-tins. Care must be taken to prevent burning.

Gingerbread makes a delicious dessert served with whipped cream.

SOFT MOLASSES GINGERBREAD

¼ cup fat	½ teaspoon salt
1 cup molasses	1 tablespoon ginger
1 tablespoon vinegar	1 cup sour milk
1 egg	2 cups flour
1 teaspoon soda	

Melt the fat, add the molasses, vinegar, and beaten egg. Mix and sift the dry ingredients and add alternately with the milk. Pour into a greased pan and bake twenty-five minutes in a moderate oven (360°-380° F.). Batter should be just thin enough so that the track left by the spoon in stirring disappears at once.

NUT CAKES

2 eggs	1 teaspoon baking-powder
½ cup molasses	½ teaspoon salt
½ cup sugar	1 tablespoon butter
1 cup flour	½ cup chopped nut-meats

Beat the eggs slightly and add the molasses and sugar. Mix and sift the flour, baking-powder and salt, and stir them into the first mixture. Add melted butter and nuts, and half fill shallow greased molds with the mixture. Place a nut-meat in the center of each. Bake in a moderate oven (360-380° F.) for twenty-five minutes.

TEA CAKES

1 tablespoon melted fat	3 teaspoons baking-powder
½ cup sugar	2 cups flour
1 egg	1 cup chopped nuts
1 cup milk	

Cream the fat with the sugar, add the beaten egg, then add the milk alternately with the sifted ingredients. Lastly add the floured nuts. Bake in greased muffin-pans at 400-425° for twenty minutes. Split each cake, butter it, and sprinkle with sugar and cinnamon or with grated maple sugar and chopped nuts. Serve hot with afternoon tea.

LITTLE CHOCOLATE CAKES

¼ cup butter	2 squares melted chocolate
1 cup sugar	1 cup pastry flour
½ cup milk	1 teaspoon baking-powder
2 eggs	1 teaspoon vanilla

Cream butter, add the sugar slowly, then the beaten egg-yolks. Melt the chocolate and add. Add flour and baking-powder sifted together, alternating with milk, and add vanilla and fold in stiffly beaten egg-whites. Bake in greased muffin-pans.

MOCHA CAKES

1 cup sifted powdered sugar	1½ cups sifted pastry flour
2 eggs	1 teaspoon baking-powder
½ cup strong coffee	⅓ teaspoon salt
	½ cup evaporated milk

Cream the sifted powdered sugar with the beaten egg-yolks; add the coffee and the milk, then the dry ingredients sifted together. Bake in a long shallow pan at 350° for twenty minutes, cut in fancy shapes as desired, cover the top and sides with mocha cream. Finely chopped nuts may be used to cover the sides, giving the effect of French pastries.

PETITS FOURS

4 eggs	1 cup flour
1 cup sugar	1½ teaspoon baking-powder
3 tablespoons cold water	¼ teaspoon salt
1½ tablespoon corn-starch	Flavoring

To the beaten yolks of the eggs, add sugar and cold water. Sift the corn-starch with the flour, baking-powder and salt. Add to first mixture. Beat well and add the stiffly beaten whites of the eggs and any flavoring desired. Bake for one-half hour in a moderate oven (350° F.) in shallow pans. When cool, cut in small circles, split, scoop out a little of the crum from the center of each and fill cavities with whipped cream or any prepared filling. Press together in pairs, dip in melted fondant, decorate with nuts, glacé fruits, and so forth, and place each little cake in a paper case.

CREAM PUFFS

1 cup boiling water	1 cup flour
½ cup butter or shortening	4 eggs

Add the boiling water to the butter or shortening, bring to a boil and stir in the flour thoroughly. Remove from the fire, let the mixture cool slightly and add the eggs one at a time, beating in each one for some time before adding the next. Drop by spoonfuls on a greased pan about two inches apart, shaping into a circular form and having the batter a little higher in the center. Bake one-half hour in a moderate oven (360° F.). If these cakes are removed from the oven before they are thoroughly done, they will fall. Take out one; if it does not fall, the others may be removed.

Cool and split partly with a sharp knife. Fill with a cream filling, whipped cream, or a fruit mixture.

Cream puffs and éclairs make an excellent foundation for a great variety of desserts. Split them open, fill with any kind of ice-cream, and cover with any sauce or combination of sauces. Replace cover, and serve immediately.

LADY FINGERS

5 tablespoons powdered sugar	½ teaspoon vanilla
3 egg-whites	½ cup flour
2 egg-yolks	¼ teaspoon salt

Add the powdered sugar to the stiffly beaten egg-whites. Add to these the two well-beaten yolks and the vanilla extract. Fold in the flour, which has been sifted twice with the salt. Line a pan with paper but do not grease it. Press the batter through a pastry bag on to it, forming strips four inches long and one inch wide. Sprinkle with powdered sugar and bake in a moderate oven (350° F.) for ten minutes.

MERINGUES AND KISSES

2 egg-whites
½ cup powdered sugar

Pinch of salt
½ teaspoon flavoring

Beat the egg-whites stiff, adding the salt. Add the sugar gradually, beating constantly, and heap in rounds or press through a pastry bag on to a wet board covered with an ungreased paper.

Bake on the board in a very slow oven (320° F.) for three-quarters of an hour. The kisses should be very light brown and quite dry. If they adhere to the paper, moisten the other side of the paper by placing it on a wet cloth, and they will slip off easily.

The smaller shapes or kisses may be stuck together in pairs with a little white of egg, and the meringues, which are usually made larger, may be scooped out and filled with ice-cream or whipped cream.

COCONUT DROPS

4 egg-whites
½ pound powdered sugar

½ teaspoon lemon extract
½ pound grated coconut

Beat the egg-whites stiff, add sugar and beat until light and white, then add the lemon extract, and enough coconut to make it as thick as can be easily stirred with a spoon. Drop on greased paper and bake at 350° F. for ten minutes.

COCONUT MACAROONS

1 egg-white
1¼ cups sweet coconut

⅓ cup thick condensed milk
½ teaspoon vanilla

Beat the egg-white until stiff, then fold it into the mixture of coconut and condensed milk. Add flavoring. Drop by spoonfuls on a greased baking-sheet and shape into cakes. Bake in a moderate oven 350° F. until lightly browned.

MOCK MACAROONS

1 egg-white   1 cup brown sugar
1 cup chopped salted nuts

Beat the sugar into the stiffly beaten egg-white, and add the nuts.
Drop by spoonfuls on a greased pan and bake in a slow oven
(320° F.) for fifteen minutes.

KORNETTES

1 egg-white   ¾ cup chopped popcorn
⅓ cup light brown sugar   ¼ teaspoon salt
2 teaspoons butter   ½ teaspoon vanilla

Beat the white of the egg very stiff and, still beating, mix in the
sugar. Melt the butter and into this stir the chopped popcorn,
salt and vanilla. Fold the two mixtures together and drop by
spoonfuls on a greased baking-sheet. Bake at 350° for fifteen
minutes.

OATMEAL JIM-JAMS

1 cup butter or shortening   1 teaspoon soda
1 cup brown sugar   ½ cup sour milk
2 cups flour   2 cups ground oatmeal
½ teaspoon salt

Cream the butter or shortening with the sugar. Sift the flour, salt
and soda and add with the oatmeal to the first mixture, alternating with the milk. If ground oatmeal is not procurable, rolled
oats may be ground in a food-chopper and measured after grind-
ing. Toss on a floured board and roll thin. Cut in rounds. Put
on greased baking-sheet and bake in a moderate oven (350° F.)
twelve to fifteen minutes. When cool, put together like sandwiches with the following filling:

¾ pound chopped dates   ½ cup boiling water
¾ cup sugar

Cook ingredients together until thick. Cool before spreading.

CAKES

FOUNDATION OR PLAIN CAKE

⅓ cup butter or shortening
1 cup sugar
2 eggs
1¾ cup flour

2 teaspoons baking-powder
½ cup milk
1 teaspoon vanilla

Cream the butter or butter substitute, add sugar and continue creaming. Add well-beaten eggs. Mix and sift the dry ingredients and add alternately with the milk. Add flavoring. Bake in layers at 380° for twenty minutes. Any good filling and frosting may be used.

The batter may be varied by adding nuts, coconut, spices, etc., and may be baked as a loaf cake.

ONE-TWO-THREE-FOUR CAKE (Measure Cake)

1 cup butter or shortening
2 cups sugar
3 cups flour
4 eggs

3 teaspoons baking-powder
1 cup milk
Flavoring

Cream the butter or shortening and sugar, add eggs. Mix and sift flour and baking-powder and add alternately with the milk. Flavor as desired. Bake as loaf or layer cake at 380-400° F. for twenty to forty-five minutes.

MAPLE-SUGAR CAKE

½ cup butter or shortening
1¼ cups maple sugar
4 teaspoons cornstarch
1½ cups flour

½ cup milk
1¼ teaspoons vanilla
4 egg-whites
2 teaspoons baking powder

Cream the butter or shortening and sugar. Sift the corn-starch and flour together several times and add to the first mixture, alternately with the milk. Add the vanilla, then fold in the stiffly beaten egg-whites. Bake in a greased loaf-cake tin in a moderate oven (380° F.) for forty-five minutes. Cover with any desired icing.

CHOCOLATE NUT CAKE

⅔ cup butter or shortening
2 cups sugar
4 eggs
1 cup mashed potatoes
2 squares chocolate
2 cups flour
3½ teaspoons baking-powder

1 teaspoon cinnamon
½ teaspoon mace
½ teaspoon grated nutmeg
½ teaspoon ground cloves
1 cup chopped nut-meats
½ cup milk

Cream the butter or shortening and one cup of sugar. In another bowl, beat the egg-yolks with the remaining cup of sugar. Combine the two mixtures. Have ready the hot mashed potatoes, which should be without lumps, add to them the melted chocolate and combine with the first mixture. Mix and sift the dry ingredients and add the nut-meats. Add to the cake mixture, alternating with the milk. Fold in the stiffly beaten whites. Bake in a loaf pan in a moderate oven (380° F.). When cool, cover with marshmallow frosting or boiled frosting. This is a large moist cake, which will keep well.

CHOCOLATE LOAF CAKE

2 tablespoons butter or shortening
1 cup sugar
2 tablespoons grated chocolate
2 cups flour

2 teaspoons baking-powder
1 cup milk
2 cups seeded raisins
12 black walnut-meats
½ teaspoon vanilla extract

Cream the butter or shortening; add the sugar and continue creaming. Melt the chocolate over hot water, and add. Mix and sift the flour and baking-powder and add alternately with the milk. Add the raisins, broken nut-meats well floured, and the flavoring. Mix well. Bake in a loaf pan 360° F. for forty-five minutes. When cool, frost with boiled or chocolate frosting.

CHOCOLATE SOUR-MILK CAKE

½ cup butter or shortening
1 cup sugar
3 eggs
½ cup sour milk

2 cups flour
⅓ teaspoon soda
⅓ cup hot water
1 square chocolate

Cream butter or shortening and sugar; add eggs well beaten, and the milk. Add sifted flour. Dissolve the soda in the hot water and add grated chocolate to this mixture. Beat the mixture smooth and put in a well-greased loaf pan. Bake in a moderate oven (380° F.) for forty-five minutes.

FUDGE CAKE

⅓ cup butter or shortening
1½ cups sugar
3 eggs
2½ cups flour
2 teaspoons baking-powder

¼ teaspoon salt
½ cup cocoa
1 cup milk
1½ cups chopped walnut-meats
1½ teaspoons vanilla

Cream the butter or shortening and sugar; add the well-beaten egg-yolks. Mix and sift the dry ingredients and add alternately with the milk. Stir in the chopped nut-meats, well floured, and add the flavoring. Fold in the stiffly beaten egg-whites. Bake in layer-cake tins in a moderate oven (380° F.) for forty-five minutes. When cold, spread chocolate frosting between layers and on top.

NUT CAKE

½ cup butter or shortening
1 cup sugar
2 cups flour

2 teaspoons baking-powder
¾ cup milk
1 cup chopped nut-meats
4 egg-whites

Cream butter or shortening and add the sugar. Mix and sift the dry ingredients and add alternately with the milk. Add nut-meats, well floured, and fold in the egg-whites. Bake in a square loaf pan at 380° F., and frost the top when cool, using any desired icing.

GOLDEN CAKE

¼ cup butter or shortening
½ cup sugar
3 egg-yolks
1 cup flour

2 teaspoons baking-powder
¼ cup milk
1 teaspoon orange extract

Cream the butter or shortening and add the sugar gradually. Beat the yolks until thick and lemon-colored. Mix and sift the dry ingredients and add to the first mixture alternately with the milk. Flavor. Bake as loaf or layer cake, in a moderate oven (380° F.) for forty-five minutes.

LADY BALTIMORE CAKE

(From a famous recipe)

6 eggs
Pinch of cream of tartar
Pinch of salt
Sugar
Flour
1 teaspoon baking-powder
2 cups milk
2 ounces grated chocolate
(about 10 tablespoons)

4 ounces granulated sugar
(about 8 tablespoons)
4 ounces almond paste
(about 8 tablespoons)
4 egg-yolks
¼ pound shredded citron
½ cup pecan nut-meats
Soft boiled frosting flavored
with vanilla

This cake is made in three parts: cake, chocolate-cream filling and nut cream.

For the cake, weigh five eggs and take their weight in sugar (about one and one-fourth cup), weigh three eggs and take their weight in flour (about one and one-half cup). Separate whites from yolks of six eggs, add cream of tartar and salt to the whites and beat until very stiff and dry. Beat the yolks as dry as possible, and add to them the sugar, then fold in the whites quickly. Sift the flour three times, with the baking-powder, and whip into the mixture. Bake about three-quarters of an hour in an oven that slowly rises in temperature, keeping a piece of paper over the top of the pan. When cold, cut into three layers, with a sharp knife.

For the chocolate cream, heat one cup of milk in a double boiler with two ounces of sugar and two ounces of almond paste, add the chocolate, melted, and the beaten yolks of two eggs. Set aside to cool.

For the nut cream, heat one cup of milk in the double boiler with two ounces of sugar and two ounces of almond paste, add the shredded citron and the pecan-meats ground in a vegetable grinder, and thicken with two egg-yolks.

When both creams are cool enough, spread the layers, using the nut filling for the bottom layer, the chocolate for the second and the boiled frosting for the top of the cake.

The almond paste may be bought at a confectioner's, or the almonds may be blanched and pounded. One and one-third cup of shelled almonds makes four ounces of paste.

*This layer cake, page 140, has a covering of chocolate frosting,
page 149, and marshmallow filling.*

*Cream cake has a filling of fruit. The garnish of whipped cream
is put on with the pastry bag.*

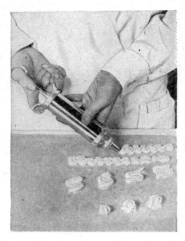

An iced cake may be made as decorative as you wish with the aid of an icing syringe and various tips.

Fill the syringe, adjust the desired tip, press the plunger and move the syringe over the iced cake.

FIG LOAF CAKE

1 cup butter or shortening	1 teaspoon cinnamon
2 cups brown sugar	½ teaspoon ground cloves
4 eggs	1 teaspoon nutmeg
3 cups flour	1 cup water
2 teaspoons baking-powder	½ pound finely cut figs
¼ teaspoon salt	2 cups chopped raisins

Cream the butter or shortening and add the sugar. Add the eggs, well beaten. Mix and sift the dry ingredients and add alternately with the water. Add figs and raisins, dredged with a little of the flour. Bake in a greased loaf pan in a slow oven (320° F.) about two hours.

MARTHA WASHINGTON FRUIT CAKE

½ pound butter or shortening	¼ teaspoon mace
1½ pounds sugar	2 cups sour cream
6 eggs	1 pound chopped raisins
1¾ pounds flour	1 pound well-cleaned currants
1 teaspoon soda	½ pound sliced citron
¼ teaspoon salt	Juice and rind of 1 lemon
1 grated nutmeg	

Cream the butter or shortening and add the sugar. Gradually add the well-beaten egg-yolks. Mix and sift the dry ingredients and add alternately with the cream. Add the raisins, currants, citron well floured, and lemon. Mix well. Fold in the stiffly beaten egg-whites. Turn into paper-lined loaf-cake pans and cover the tops with greased paper. Bake slowly at 320° F., about two and one-half hours.

WEDDING CAKE

4 pounds raisins	½ ounce ground cloves
3 pounds currants	1 pound butter or shortening
1 pound citron	1 pound brown sugar
1 pound flour	10 eggs
½ ounce mace	2 cups molasses
½ ounce cinnamon	¼ cup strong coffee
½ ounce nutmeg	

Seed the raisins and chop them. Wash the currants and remove
e stems by vigorously rubbing them in a coarse towel,

then shake in a colander. Cut the citron into small pieces. Sift the flour and spices together so that they are thoroughly mixed. Rub the butter or shortening and sugar together until they are foamy. Beat the yolks until they are thick and lemon-colored, then add them to the fat and sugar. Add the molasses and coffee and stir well. Sift a little of the flour over the fruit and add the rest of it to the cake mixture, beating until smooth. Add the fruit and lastly fold in the beaten egg-whites. Put in deep cake pans lined with greased paper and bake in a slow oven (320° F.) for three or four hours. When cold, frost the top with boiled frosting, maple-sugar frosting, brown-sugar frosting, or coffee frosting.

APPLE-SAUCE CAKE

⅓ cup butter or shortening
1 cup sugar
1½ cups thick sweetened apple sauce
2 cups flour

1 teaspoon soda
Pinch of salt
Spices to taste
1 cup raisins

Cream butter or shortening and sugar together, then add the apple sauce. Mix and sift flour, soda, and spices, then the raisins. Mix well. Bake in well-greased loaf pan at 380° F. for about forty-five minutes.

TRUE SPONGE CAKE

6 eggs
1 cup sugar
1 tablespoon lemon-juice

½ teaspoon grated lemon-rind
1 cup flour

Separate the whites and yolks of the eggs, beat the yolks until thick and lemon-colored, add the sugar gradually, then add the lemon-juice and rind. Cut and fold in the sifted flour and cut and fold in the stiffly beaten egg-whites. Bake in an ungreased pan in a very moderate oven, 300° to 350° F.

MOCK SPONGE CAKE

3 eggs
1 cup sugar
½ cup cold water
1½ cups flour

1½ teaspoons baking-powder
¼ teaspoon salt
½ teaspoon vanilla

Beat the eggs, add the sugar and beat well. Add the water, alternating with the sifted dry ingredients, then the vanilla. Bake in an ungreased pan in a moderate oven (350° F.).

ANGEL CAKE

9 egg-whites
1 teaspoon cream of tartar
1 cup sugar
⅞ cup flour
⅛ teaspoon salt
1 teaspoon vanilla

Beat the whites of the eggs to a froth, add the cream of tartar and beat till the eggs are stiff but not dry, then gradually add the sugar (which has been sifted twice), beating after additions. Sift the flour with the salt five times and fold it into the mixture. Add the vanilla. Bake in an ungreased angel-cake tin in a very moderate oven (250-320° F.) for forty-five minutes. Be careful not to jar or disturb while baking. Remove from the oven, turn the pan upside down on a wire netting or with a knife handle or some other small article inserted under the edge of the pan to permit steam to escape, and let it stand until the cake falls out. Ice placed on the bottom of the tin will hasten the release of the cake.

MOCK ANGEL CAKE

1 cup sugar
1 cup flour
¼ teaspoon salt
2 teaspoons baking-powder
1 cup milk
2 egg-whites

Put dry ingredients into a bowl, mixing and sifting well. Scald the milk in a double boiler. Stir quickly into the dry ingredients, and take care to have no lumps. Beat the egg-whites until stiff and fold them into the batter. Bake in a loaf pan in a moderate oven (350° F.) for forty-five minutes.

JELLY ROLL

3 eggs
¾ cup sugar
5 tablespoons milk
1½ cups flour
1 teaspoon baking-powder
¼ teaspoon salt
1 tablespoon lemon extract
½ pint jelly

Beat the yolks of the eggs until light, then add the sugar. Stir well and add the flour and baking-powder sifted together, alternately with the milk. Add flavoring. Grease a long shallow pan of the size usually used in roasting meats. The batter should be one-fourth inch deep, for if it is thicker the cake will not roll easily. Bake six to eight minutes in a moderate oven (350° F.), watching closely, as it bakes quickly. When done, remove from the oven, and when cool enough to handle, turn out on to a cloth. Cut off the side crusts, spread the jelly over the surface, roll up and wrap the cloth about it to keep it in shape. If the cake was spread too thick in the pan and will not roll, cut it into three parts and lay one upon the other with jelly between. This makes a most delicious layer cake. In this case, frost with a boiled frosting, and sprinkle with a layer of coconut.

CAKE FILLINGS AND FROSTINGS

CHOCOLATE FILLING

Yolks 2 eggs
1½ cups sugar
½ cup milk
1 tablespoon butter

4 squares chocolate
2 teaspoons vanilla
Few grains of salt

Melt chocolate. Beat very light. Add sugar and salt and continue beating. Add milk and butter. Cook over flame until it boils, stirring all the time. When it has boiled hard for one minute, take from fire, add melted chocolate and vanilla, and beat until thick enough to spread and hold its shape.

COCONUT FILLING

½ cup milk
1½ cups shredded coconut
2 egg-whites

4 tablespoons confectioners' sugar

Warm the milk, pour it over the coconut and soak until well softened, usually one-half hour. Beat the egg-whites stiff and add the sugar gradually. Spread a thin coating of the egg and sugar mixture on the layer, then spread a covering of the moistened coconut. To what is left of the filling, add enough confectioners' sugar to thicken, stir in the remaining coconut and spread the mixture thickly over the top. Sprinkle the whole cake with dry coconut.

CREAM FILLING

1 tablespoon corn-starch
1 cup milk
1 egg-yolk
⅛ teaspoon salt

1 teaspoon vanilla
2 tablespoons confectioners' sugar
½ teaspoon butter

Mix the corn-starch with two tablespoons of the milk. Heat the rest of the milk in a double boiler and stir the corn-starch paste slowly into it. Stir the mixture until it is smooth and cook it for fifteen minutes. Add the beaten egg-yolk and cook two minutes longer. Remove from the fire and add the salt, sugar and butter. Beat well. Add flavoring. Cool before spreading on layers of cake.

LEMON FILLING

2½ tablespoons flour
½ cup cold water
1 egg-yolk
1 cup sugar

Juice and grated rind of 1 lemon
1 teaspoon butter

Make a smooth paste of the flour and two tablespoons of the cold water. Cook the rest of the water, the sugar, grated lemon-rind and butter. When the sugar is dissolved and mixture boiling, stir in the flour mixture slowly. Cook until clear and smooth, about fifteen minutes. Add lemon-juice and beaten egg-yolk and cook two minutes. Cool before spreading on cake.

PRUNE FILLING

¼ pound prunes
2 tablespoons gelatin
4 tablespoons cold water
½ cup sugar

½ cup rhubarb or canned pine-apple-juice
½ cup whipped cream

Wash the prunes, soak overnight in water to cover, and cook slowly until soft. Remove pits and rub pulp through a coarse sieve. Soak the gelatin in cold water. When soft, add it to the boiling prune pulp and stir until the gelatin dissolves. Add sugar and fruit-juice. When the filling has cooled, fold in the whipped cream.

CONFECTIONERS' FROSTING

1 egg-white
½ cup confectioners' sugar

½ teaspoon vanilla

Beat the egg-white stiff and add the sugar gradually; continue beating until the mixture is smooth and light. Add flavoring.

BOILED FROSTING

1 cup sugar
½ cup water

1 egg-white
½ teaspoon vanilla

Cook the sugar and water together, stirring until the sugar has dissolved. Then, without stirring, cook until the sirup will form a thread when dropped from the tip of a spoon (or until it reaches 238° F.). Remove from the fire and cool while beating the egg-white stiff, then pour the sirup in a thin stream over the stiff white, beating the mixture constantly until thick enough to spread.

BROWN-SUGAR FROSTING

1 cup brown sugar
½ cup water
2 egg-whites

1 teaspoon vanilla or ½ teaspoon lemon extract

Make a sirup of the sugar and water and cook to the soft-ball stage (238° F.). Remove from the fire and cool while the egg-whites are beaten, then pour the sirup in a thin stream on to the stiff whites, beating the mixture constantly until thick enough to spread. Add the flavoring. Chopped nuts may be stirred into the frosting just before spreading.

CHOCOLATE FROSTING

1 square chocolate
3 tablespoons sugar
1 tablespoon water
1 egg-white

8 tablespoons confectioners' sugar
½ tablespoon vanilla

Cook the chocolate, sugar and water together, stirring until the mixture is smooth and glossy. Beat the white of the egg enough to thin it, but not to make it frothy; add the sugar, stir until smooth and light, then add the chocolate mixture and vanilla. Cool before spreading on the cake.

COCONUT FROSTING

2 cups sugar
½ cup water
1 teaspoon butter

1 teaspoon vanilla extract or ½ teaspoon lemon extract
½ cup shredded or grated coconut

Boil sugar and water to the soft-ball stage (238° F.), then add butter and cook until thick enough to spread. Add flavoring. When cool spread on cake and sprinkle coconut over the top.

CANDIES

CHOCOLATE FUDGE

2 cups sugar
1 or 2 squares chocolate
⅛ teaspoon cream of tartar or
  2 tablespoons corn sirup or
  glucose

⅔ cup milk
1 teaspoon vanilla
1 tablespoon butter

Mix the sugar, milk, grated chocolate, cream of tartar or corn sirup and boil rather slowly, stirring until the ingredients are well blended. Boil to the soft-ball stage, or 236° F. Remove from the stove, add the butter, but do not stir it in. When lukewarm, add the vanilla and beat until it creams; that is, until the shiny appearance disappears and the fudge holds its shape. Spread it in a buttered pan and when it hardens mark it into squares.

MAPLE FUDGE

2½ cups maple sugar
1 cup milk

½ cup boiling water
1 cup broken nut-meats

Break the maple sugar into small pieces and heat it in a saucepan with the water. When it is dissolved, add the milk. Boil to the soft-ball stage, or 236° F. Remove from the fire and cool. When it is lukewarm, beat until it creams and add the nut-meats. Spread it in a buttered pan and when it hardens mark it into squares.

FUDGE WITH MARSHMALLOW CREAM

2 cups sugar
2 squares chocolate
1 cup water
½ teaspoon salt

4 tablespoons marshmallow
  cream
1 teaspoon vanilla

Put the sugar, water, grated chocolate and salt into a saucepan and stir until the sugar is dissolved. Boil slowly to the soft-ball stage, or 236° F. Remove from the fire, pour it over the marsh-mallow cream in a bowl, but do not stir. When it is lukewarm, add the vanilla and beat until it is creamy. Pour into buttered pans and when it hardens mark it into squares.

PENOCHE

3 cups brown sugar
1 cup milk
1 tablespoon butter

1 teaspoon vanilla
1 cup nut-meats

Put the sugar and milk into a saucepan and cook to the soft-ball stage, or 236° F. Remove from the fire, add butter and vanilla, and cool without stirring. When it is lukewarm, beat until it is creamy. Stir in the broken nut-meats. Hickory nuts or English walnuts are especially nice. Pour into a buttered pan and when it hardens mark into squares.

FONDANT

2 cups granulated sugar
1 cup water
1 teaspoon vanilla

2 tablespoons corn sirup or ⅛ teaspoon cream of tartar

Put the sugar, corn sirup and water in a saucepan and heat slowly. Do not let it begin to boil until the sugar is dissolved. Wash down the sides of the pan with a fork wrapped in a damp cloth or else cover and cook for two or three minutes so that the steam will carry down the crystals that have been thrown on the side of the pan. Remove the cover and continue to boil slowly without stirring to the soft-ball stage, or 238° F. While cooking, keep the cover on part of the time so the steam can help to keep the crystals washed down.

Remove from the fire and pour at once on large platters or slabs which have been wet with water, and let it stand until it is lukewarm. Cream thoroughly; then knead with the hands until it is smooth and free from lumps. Fondant is better if allowed to ripen for several days. It may be wrapped in waxed paper and put in a tightly covered jar.

WINTERGREEN CREAMS

Melt a portion of fondant in the upper part of a double boiler until it is soft enough to drop from a spoon. It may be necessary to add a few drops of hot water. Color it with red vegetable coloring to a delicate pink. Flavor with oil of wintergreen. Stir until it is creamy. Drop from a teaspoon on oiled paper.

VANILLA CARAMELS

2 cups sugar	1 teaspoon vanilla
½ cup corn sirup	4 tablespoons butter
½ cup milk	1 cup cream or condensed milk

Cook the ingredients, except the vanilla, to the firm-ball stage, or 246° F. Remove from the fire, add the vanilla and pour into a buttered pan. When it is cold, turn it out of the pan and cut it into squares.

MOLASSES TAFFY

2 cups molasses	⅛ teaspoon soda
1 cup granulated sugar	4 tablespoons butter
¾ cup water	½ teaspoon vanilla

Cook the molasses, sugar and water slowly to the hard-ball stage, or 260° F., stirring during the latter part of the cooking to prevent its burning. Remove from the fire, add the butter, soda and vanilla and stir enough to mix. Pour into a greased pan and, when cool enough to handle, pull it into a long rope and cut with scissors into small pieces.

NOUGAT

2 cups sugar	1 teaspoon vanilla
⅓ cup corn sirup	1½ cups nut-meats
1 cup water	½ cup candied cherries
4 egg-whites	

Boil together one-half the sugar, half of the water and half of the corn sirup to the crack stage, or 280° F. Remove the sirup from the fire and pour it slowly over the well-beaten whites and continue beating until it is cool. While beating, cook the remaining half of the ingredients to the crack stage, or 280° F. Remove and add at once to the first mixture, beating while adding. When cool, add the vanilla, nut-meats and candied cherries and pour into buttered pans. Smooth over the surface and let it stand overnight before cutting. In the morning cut and wrap in oiled paper.

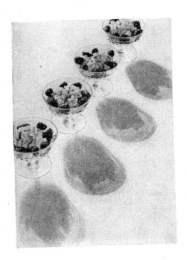

Who would not be tempted
by ice cream with fruit,
above, or with nuts and
chocolate sauce, below?

There is something about
the very shape of a par-
fait glass that makes the
contents doubly tempting

For mousse, above, cream
must be whipped; but for
ice-cream, below, this is
not necessary, page 170

Biscuit glacé, page 155, is
particularly well suited to
freezing in the trays of
the mechanical refrigerator

POPCORN BALLS

3 quarts popped corn
1 cup sugar
1/3 cup white corn sirup

1 cup water
1/4 teaspoon salt
1 teaspoon lemon or vanilla

Discard all imperfect kernels of corn. Put the corn into a large pan. Cook sugar, sirup and water to the crack stage, or 270° F. Add flavoring and salt. Pour slowly over the corn, stirring with a spoon so that all kernels will be evenly coated. Shape the corn into balls and lay on waxed paper. Wrap in waxed paper, if desirable.

PEANUT BRITTLE

2 cups granulated sugar
1 pint chopped peanuts

1 teaspoon salt

Put the granulated sugar into an iron frying-pan and heat slowly until the sugar is melted and turns a light brown, or slightly above 300° F., stirring constantly. Have in readiness the finely chopped peanuts, sprinkled with the salt. Place these in a buttered tin, warm slightly and pour over them the melted sugar.

GLACÉ FRUITS

2 cups sugar
1 cup water
Fruit

2 tablespoons lemon-juice or
1/8 teaspoon cream of tartar

Make a sirup of the sugar and water. Boil, without stirring, to the hard-crack stage, or 300° F. Remove the saucepan from the fire and set it in an outer pan of boiling water to prevent the sirup from hardening. Add the lemon-juice. Dip the fruits, one at a time, into the hot sirup. Remove and place on an oiled paper to dry.

FRUIT DESSERTS

STUFFED PEACHES

Pare large peaches and cut a slice from the top of each. Remove the pits without breaking the fruit and fill hollows with any chopped fruit, such as apples, citron, raisins, or with nuts. Sprinkle with sugar and a little cinnamon or nutmeg. Pour custard over the peaches and bake; or serve cold soft custard with the chilled fruit.

FRESH-FRUIT CUP

½ pineapple	3 oranges
1 cup strawberries	2 tablespoons lemon-juice
3 bananas	Sugar

Peel and dice the pineapple, bananas and oranges. Wash and hull the strawberries. Mix all together, with the lemon-juice and sugar, and set on ice until very cold.

MACEDOINE OF FRUIT

3 peaches	½ cup diced watermelon
3 pears	1 cup raspberries
½ cup diced pineapple	⅓ cup sugar

Pare and slice peaches and pears, cut pineapple and melon in small pieces, mix fruit and sugar, and chill for one hour. Serve in glasses, adding one tablespoon whipped cream to each glass just before serving. A berry or piece of pineapple placed on the cream gives color to the dish.

BLUSHING APPLES

6 red apples	1½ cups water
1½ cups sugar	Whipped cream

Core the apples. Cook in sirup made of sugar and water, turning so that they will cook evenly until they are tender. Carefully remove the skin, scraping the red pulp from it and basting on the sides of the apple. Put the apples in a serving-dish. Reduce the sirup to one cup, and add the grated rind and juice of one orange, the juice of one lemon, and if desired, nuts, candied orange-peel, or raisins. Pour sirup over apples and serve with whipped cream.

BAKED STUFFED APPLES

6 large tart red apples
1 cup chopped bananas
1 cup chopped cranberries
1 cup sugar
1 teaspoon cinnamon
Chopped nut-meats
Whipped cream

Cut off the stem end of the apples, but do not peel them. Remove all the core and part of the pulp, leaving the walls of the cup about three-fourths inch thick. Mix bananas, cranberries, sugar, and cinnamon. Fill the cavities in the apples with this mixture, cover with chopped nut-meats, and bake in the oven until tender. Serve cold with a spoonful of whipped cream on top of each apple.

STUFFED BAKED PEARS

Pare and core large pears and stuff with seeded dates, raisins or chopped nuts with some tart marmalade or shredded coconut. Place close together in a baking-dish, cover bottom of pan with water and bake slowly until tender.

MERINGUED PEARS

6 large pears
6 tablespoons sugar
Grated lemon-rind
Candied ginger
3 egg-whites
1/4 cup powdered sugar

Pare and core the pears, place them in a baking-dish and fill the centers with one tablespoon sugar, a little grated lemon-rind or candied ginger. Add three or four tablespoons of water and bake until tender. Cover them with a meringue made with the stiffly beaten whites of eggs and the sugar. Brown quickly.

GELATIN AND CREAM DESSERTS

GRAPEFRUIT À LA ST. PATRICK

1 ounce (2 tablespoons) gran-
    ulated gelatin
½ cup cold water
½ cup boiling water
Fresh mint

¾ cup sugar
1 cup ice-water
2 cups grapefruit pulp and
    juice
Maraschino cherries

Keep the grapefruit skins, in halves. Simmer a few sprigs of fresh mint in the boiling water until the flavor is extracted. Follow the standard directions for making jelly. When jelly is firm, cut it into cubes, pile the cubes in the grapefruit shells and garnish with sprigs of mint and cherries.

RAISIN EGGS

1 ounce (2 tablespoons) gran-
    ulated gelatin
½ cup cold water
½ cup boiling water
¼ cup sugar

3 tablespoons lemon-juice
2½ cups pineapple-juice and
    pulp
1 cup steamed and chopped
    raisins

Follow directions on package for making jelly. When it is beginning to set, add the raisins. Pour into molds the shape of half eggs or into large spoons and place in a cold place until firm, then remove from the molds and form into the shape of eggs by putting halves together with a little soft gelatin. Let stand in a cold place to stiffen.

JELLIED PRUNES

1 ounce (2 tablespoons) gran-
    ulated gelatin
½ cup cold water
½ cup boiling water
¾ cup sugar

2 tablespoons lemon-juice
½ pound prunes
2 cups water
Cream

Wash the prunes, soak overnight in the water and cook until tender in the same water. Drain, reserving the liquid. Remove the stones and cut the prunes in quarters. Mix prune-juice and pulp and add boiling water, if necessary, to make two cups. Chill and add lemon-juice. Follow directions on package for making jelly. This may be served with whipped or plain cream.

MONT BLANC

1 pound large chestnuts (Italian chestnuts are best for this)	½ teaspoon salt ¾ cup sugar Whipped cream

Put the chestnuts into the oven for a moment, until the shell and inner skin can be easily removed. Boil the skinned chestnuts in water with the salt and three tablespoons of the sugar, until they are very tender. Add one-half cup sugar to the water and chestnuts and let stand until thoroughly cold. Remove chestnuts from this sirup and run them through a potato-ricer on to a platter, mounding it high. Save a few of the finest whole pieces to decorate the dish. Top it all with a spoonful of sweetened whipped cream, and put a border of whipped cream around the edge of the dish, dotting it with the whole nuts here and there.

MACAROON BISQUE

1 cup heavy cream Powdered sugar Vanilla	18 macaroons 6 Maraschino cherries

Whip a cup of cream until stiff, sweeten with powdered sugar and flavor lightly with vanilla. Stir in six macaroons broken in small pieces, but not powdered. Pile in sherbet glasses with a border of the whole macaroons and decorate with marshmallows or Maraschino cherries. This is an excellent emergency dessert.

PINEAPPLE AMBROSIA

1 fresh pineapple ½ pound marshmallows 1 cup heavy cream	2 tablespoons sugar 1½ tablespoons lemon-juice

Shred the pineapple with a fork. Cut the marshmallows into small pieces, using a pair of scissors. Mix the pineapple and marshmallows and let stand on ice until thoroughly chilled. Just before serving, whip the cream and add the sugar to it. Add lemon-juice to·the pineapple mixture and then fold in the whipped cream. Serve immediately in individual glasses or in a large dessert dish.

PEACH FLUFF

1 cup sugar

1 cup thick cream

2 egg-whites

4 cups sliced peaches

Add half the sugar to the cream, stir until the sugar is dissolved, and then add the whites of the eggs beaten stiff. Place the sliced peaches in a dish, sprinkle them with the remainder of the sugar, pour on the cream mixture, and serve at once. The success of this depends upon its being thoroughly chilled when served. The cream, eggs and fruit should be placed on ice at least two hours before the dish is to be prepared, and the latter should be sent to the table as quickly as possible, being kept in the ice-box until needed.

Apple fluff or berry fluff may be made in the same way.

FIG PUFF

1 cup cream

1 egg-white

1 tablespoon grapefruit marmalade

2 tablespoons powdered sugar

Chopped figs

Maraschino cherries

Shredded almonds

Whip the cream until thick. Beat the egg-white until stiff, then combine with the cream and add the sugar and marmalade. Stir chopped figs into the mixture until it becomes very thick. Pack in long-stemmed glasses. This may be garnished by sprinkling the top with macaroon crums. Arrange a half maraschino cherry with radiating strips of almonds in the center of each.

PUDDINGS

PRUNE SOUFFLÉ

12 large prunes
3 egg-whites

3 tablespoons powdered sugar

Soak prunes overnight and stew in the same water until tender.
Remove stones and mash to a smooth pulp. Beat the egg-whites
until stiff, fold in the sugar and then the prune pulp. Turn into a
greased baking-dish and bake in a slow oven (300° F.) about
twenty minutes. Serve at once with cream, soft custard or any
desired sauce.

CHOCOLATE SOUFFLÉ

1 cup scalded milk
3 tablespoons flour
2 ounces grated chocolate

1 tablespoon fat
⅓ cup sugar
3 eggs

Make a sauce of the milk, flour, chocolate, fat and sugar. Stir
in the egg yolks, and fold in the beaten egg-whites. Proceed as
in Prune Soufflé.

BROWN BETTY

¼ cup melted butter
1 pint bread-crumbs from center of loaf
1 pint sliced apples

½ cup fruit-juice or water
½ cup sugar or molasses
Juice and grated rind of lemon
or orange

Arrange alternate layers of buttered bread-crumbs and thinly sliced
apples in a pudding-dish, sprinkle with sugar and a little cinnamon
or other spices. Finish with crumbs and pour mixed molasses and
water or fruit-juice over all. Cover and bake for one-half hour,
remove the cover and bake three-fourths of an hour more.

Stewed peaches, apricots or rhubarb make a good substitute for
the apples in this pudding.

PEACH BETTY

6 large peaches
4 tablespoons butter
⅔ cup raspberry-juice

½ cup fine bread- or cake-crums
2 tablespoons sugar

Cut the peaches in halves, removing the stones. Place the halves in a baking-dish, hollow side up, and put one teaspoon butter or butter substitute in each half. Pour half of the fruit-juice over the peaches; sprinkle with crums and sugar, arrange the second layer and bake, basting occasionally with the remaining juice. Serve the peaches in the hot baking-dish.

ORANGE AND RICE

Pare oranges, cut in halves crosswise and remove the core. Cook the halves in a sirup made from equal parts of sugar and water, to which a little lemon-juice has been added, until they are tender but not broken. Place around a mound of boiled rice and pour the sirup over the whole. Serve with plain or whipped cream, or a custard sauce.

CREAM RICE PUDDING

3 tablespoons rice
1 tablespoon sugar
1 quart milk

½ teaspoon salt
½ teaspoon cinnamon or nutmeg

Wash the rice thoroughly, add the other ingredients and pour into a greased baking-dish. Bake for three hours in a slow oven, stirring several times during the first hour. The mixture should not boil. Serve either hot or cold.

This is the old-fashioned creamy pudding which has such a delicious flavor because of the long slow cooking. One-half cup of raisins may be added, if desired.

INDIAN PUDDING

1 quart milk
⅓ cup corn-meal
½ cup raisins
½ teaspoon cinnamon

½ cup brown sugar
½ teaspoon salt
½ teaspoon ginger
1 egg

Place the milk in a double boiler and when it is scalding hot add the meal, moistened with cold water, and stir constantly to avoid lumps. Cook for twenty minutes. Turn into a pudding-dish and add all the other ingredients except the egg. Stir well and when the mass has cooked somewhat stir in the beaten egg. Bake for one hour in a rather slow oven and serve hot with hard sauce or any desired sauce. One-half cup dates or figs may be used instead of the raisins.

BREAD PUDDING

2 cups stale but not dry bread	2 eggs
1 quart milk	½ cup sugar
¼ teaspoon salt	1 teaspoon vanilla

Soak the bread in the milk until it is very soft, then mash it fine. Heat together until nearly boiling. Beat the eggs until light and add to them the sugar, salt and vanilla. When well mixed, stir this into the bread and milk, pour the whole into an earthenware baking-dish, set in a pan of water, and bake three-fourths of an hour in a rather slow oven.

For chocolate bread pudding, melt two squares of chocolate over hot water and add this to the soaked bread and milk.

For bread pudding with raisins, add one-half cup raisins.

COCONUT PUDDING

½ cup bread-crums	3 tablespoons sugar
½ cup coconut	½ teaspoon salt
2 cups milk	1 tablespoon butter
1 egg	

Soak the bread and coconut in the milk until soft, then mash and add the sugar, salt and melted fat. Beat the white and yolk of the egg separately; add the yolk to the mixture, then fold in the white. Pour into a greased baking-dish, set in a pan of hot water and bake in a moderate oven about thirty minutes.

QUEEN OF PUDDINGS

2 cups stale but not dry bread-crums	½ cup sugar
	Currant jelly or plum jam
1 quart scalded milk	2 tablespoons sugar for
3 eggs	meringue

Soak the crums in the hot milk until soft; then add the egg-yolks mixed with the sugar, pour into a baking-dish set in a pan of water, and bake in a moderate oven about an hour, or until custard is set. When cool, spread a thick layer of the jelly or jam over the top. Beat the egg-whites until stiff, add the sugar gradually and beat until stiff, spread this meringue on top of the jam and place in the oven until a delicate brown. Serve hot or cold, with cream.

ORANGE AND MACAROON PUDDING

⅓ pound almond macaroons   ½ cup sugar
1 pint milk   2 oranges
4 eggs

Soak the almond macaroons in the milk until soft. Beat the eggs and add to them the sugar and the grated rind of one orange. Do not grate in any of the white pith, as it spoils the flavor. Stir the mixture carefully into the macaroons and add the juice of two oranges. Pour into an oiled mold and set on a stand or ring in a kettle of boiling water. Simmer steadily for an hour. Serve hot with orange sauce.

FRUIT SHORTCAKE

2 cups flour   ⅓ cup shortening
4 teaspoons baking-powder   ¾ cup milk
½ teaspoon salt   Butter
1 tablespoon sugar

Mix and sift the dry ingredients and work in the shortening with the fingers or a knife. Gradually add enough milk to make a soft dough, mixing with a knife. Toss the dough on to a floured board and tap and roll to one-half inch thickness. Bake in sheets for a large shortcake or cut with a biscuit cutter for individual shortcakes. Bake in a hot oven for twelve minutes. When done, split into two parts, butter and put sweetened fruit between the layers and on top. Serve hot with cream.

Any fresh berries, peaches, oranges, bananas, or stewed fruits, fresh or dried, may be used for shortcake.

NEW ENGLAND PANDOWDY

Fill a deep earthen or porcelain-lined pudding dish with peeled and cored tart apples. Add one or two tablespoons water to make a little juice, sprinkle with sugar, season with nutmeg or cinnamon and cover with a baking-powder biscuit crust. Bake in a moderate oven (350° F.) for 40 minutes, and serve with a sauce of thick cream well sweetened with ordinary sugar or scraped maple sugar. Any sweetened stewed, canned or fresh fruit may be used instead of the apples.

STEAMED PUDDINGS

SUET PUDDING

3 cups sifted flour	1 teaspoon salt
1 teaspoon soda	1 cup suet
1 teaspoon cinnamon	1 cup sour milk
1 teaspoon cloves	1 cup molasses
½ teaspoon grated nutmeg	1 cup raisins

Mix and sift the dry ingredients, keeping one-half cup of flour to sift over the raisins. Chop the suet fine and add it to the milk and molasses. Combine the two mixtures and add the raisins which have been dredged with flour. Grease pudding molds or baking-powder cans and fill two-thirds full of the mixture. Cover and steam for three hours. Serve with hard sauce or any desired liquid sauce.

STEAMED CHOCOLATE PUDDING

2 cups flour	½ cup hot mashed potatoes
4½ teaspoons baking-powder	1 egg
¼ teaspoon salt	2½ squares chocolate
1 cup corn sirup	3 tablespoons butter
½ cup water	

Mix and sift the flour, baking-powder and salt. Mix the sirup with the water and add to the flour mixture. Stir in the mashed potatoes and the beaten egg. Add the chocolate, which has been melted over hot water, and the melted fat. Mix well, pour into greased individual molds and steam two hours. Serve with any desired sauce.

STEAMED CHERRY PUDDING

2 cups cherries	2½ cups flour
½ cup shortening	4 teaspoons baking-powder
1 cup sugar	1 cup milk
2 eggs	

Cream the fat and sugar and add the beaten eggs. Sift together the flour and baking-powder and add to the first mixture alternately with the milk. The cherries should be stoned and the juice drained off. Stir the cherries into the dough, turn it into greased individual molds and steam for one hour. Serve with a cherry sauce.

DATE PUDDING

1 pound dates	1 egg
½ pound beef suet	½ cup milk
3 cups bread-crums	4 tablespoons flour
¾ cup sugar	2 teaspoons baking-powder

Chop the dates and suet very fine. Mix the suet with the bread-crums. Add the dates and the sugar. Stir in the egg, add milk, and flour in which has been sifted the baking-powder. Put in a greased mold and steam for three hours. Serve with any desired sauce.

ENGLISH PLUM PUDDING

1 pound chopped suet	2 cups crums
2 pounds raisins	1 teaspoon mixed spices
1 pound currants	2 cups brown sugar
1 pound mixed peel	8 eggs
2 cups flour	

Mix the suet, the fruit and the chopped peel and dredge with some of the flour. Mix together the remaining flour, crums, spices and sugar, and add the well-beaten eggs. Stir the fruit and suet into this mixture and mix the whole thoroughly. Put into greased molds or into pudding cloths. Drop into a kettle of boiling water and boil from five to seven hours, according to the size of the pudding. Serve with hard sauce or any desired liquid sauce.

PEAR CONDÉ

1 cup rice	3 pears
2 cups boiling water	1 quart raspberries or straw-
1 teaspoon salt	berries
1 cup milk	1 cup sugar

Wash the rice and cook it in the boiling water until the water is absorbed, then add the salt and milk and continue cooking until the rice is soft. Put into small molds and chill. Turn out and serve on a platter surrounded by halves of pears. Fill the pear cavities with one-half the fresh raspberries or strawberries, crushed and sweetened. Pour the remainder of the crushed, sweetened berries over the rice and pears.

PEASANT GIRL WITH A VEIL

2 cups dried crums   1 cup tart jam   Whipped cream

This is a delicious Danish pudding. Crumble bits of graham or
rye bread to make fine crums. Add a little sugar to the crums
and heat them in slow oven until they are very dry. Cool and
mix with any kind of jam, preferably a tart jam like apricot or
plum. Mold, chill and serve with whipped cream.

FRUIT CHARLOTTE

Line cups with triangular pieces of sponge cake and chocolate
cake, alternating. Fill the center with slices of orange and peach.
Chill, turn out on a serving-plate and surround with whipped
cream and blackberries. Put a spoonful of whipped cream on
top and serve very cold.

PLAIN SOFT CUSTARD

2 cups scalded milk   4 tablespoons sugar
2 whole eggs or 4 egg-yolks ½ teaspoon vanilla
⅛ teaspoon salt

Scald the milk in the top of the double boiler. Beat together
slightly the eggs, sugar and salt. Add the hot milk to the egg
mixture, mix thoroughly and return to the top of the double
boiler. Cook over hot water, stirring constantly until the egg
coats the spoon.

WAYS OF SERVING SOFT CUSTARD

Soft custard may be served in sherbet cups, frappé glasses or
deep sauce dishes, garnished with whipped cream and pieces of
tart jelly.

It may be poured over fresh fruit.

It may be poured over lady fingers or sponge cake and may
then be garnished with meringue or whipped cream.

It may be served as a sauce for most gelatin dishes.

It is an excellent foundation for ice-creams.

If fresh milk is not available for custard making, an unsweetened canned milk or milk powder may be used with excellent
results.

PUDDING SAUCES

HOT CHOCOLATE SAUCE

1½ cups sugar
½ cup water
¼ cup rich milk or water

4 squares unsweetened chocolate
½ teaspoon vanilla

Let sugar and water boil in a saucepan for five minutes. Cool partly and gradually stir in the chocolate which has been melted over hot water. Add the vanilla. Place in a double boiler or in a pan over hot water until ready to serve. At the last moment, add the milk. (If to be used with ice-cream, use water instead of milk.)

HOT MAPLE SAUCE

½ cup water
½ cup English walnut-meats

1 pound (2 cups) maple sugar or 2 cups brown sugar

Add the water to the maple sugar and boil until it reaches the "thread" stage. Add the English walnut-meats broken into small pieces. This sauce is good with vanilla ice-cream, blanc mange or custard.

LEMON SAUCE

½ cup sugar
1 tablespoon corn-starch
2 tablespoons lemon-juice

Nutmeg
2 tablespoons butter
1 cup boiling water

Mix the sugar and corn-starch, add the boiling water and a pinch of salt and boil until thick and clear. Continue cooking over hot water for twenty minutes. Beat in the butter, the lemon-juice and nutmeg. A grating of lemon-rind may be added.

FOAMY SAUCE

½ cup butter
1 cup confectioners' sugar
1 egg

2 tablespoons hot water
1 teaspoon vanilla

Cream the butter and gradually add the sugar, the egg, well beaten, and the hot water. Heat over hot water, beating continually until it thickens. Add the vanilla and serve.

PLUM PUDDING SAUCE

¼ cup butter
1 cup powdered sugar
2 tablespoons cider

2 eggs
½ cup rich milk or cream

Cream the butter and powdered sugar. Add the cider and the well-beaten yolks of the eggs. When well mixed, stir in the milk or cream. Cook in a double boiler until it is as thick as a custard and then gradually pour it into the beaten whites of the eggs, beating constantly.

HARD SAUCE

⅓ cup butter
1 cup powdered sugar

1 teaspoon vanilla or other flavoring

Cream the butter until very soft, then add the sugar and the flavoring. Set in a cool place until required for use. A grating of lemon-rind or nutmeg, or a sprinkle of powdered cinnamon may be used instead of vanilla. Cream or milk may be added, with more sugar to make more sauce. This sauce may be used with a hot pudding of any kind.

Granulated sugar, brown sugar or maple sugar may be substituted for the powdered sugar.

BERRY SAUCE

2 cups berries
1 tablespoon butter
1½ cups powdered sugar

1 tablespoon granulated sugar
1 egg-white

The small fruits, such as raspberries, blackberries or strawberries, make most satisfactory sauce for puddings. Place the berries in a bowl, add a tablespoon of granulated sugar and mash slightly to draw out the juices, setting the bowl in a moderately warm room. Beat the butter to a cream, add the powdered sugar and when thoroughly mixed add the beaten white of the egg. Combine with the mashed berries just before serving. Serve with ice-cream, berry puddings or cottage pudding.

ICE-CREAMS AND FROZEN DESSERTS

AMERICAN ICE-CREAM

1 pint milk
2 tablespoons flour
2 tablespoons water
¾ cup sugar

2 egg-yolks
1 cup heavy cream
1 teaspoon vanilla

Scald the milk, stirring constantly. Mix the flour and cold water to a smooth paste and add to it slowly the scalded milk, continuing the stirring. When thickened, cook over hot water for about fifteen minutes. Add sugar and beaten egg-yolks and cook two minutes. Strain the custard through a fine sieve and, when cold, add the cream and vanilla and freeze. This makes a smooth, rich cream.

For variation, use dark-brown sugar or maple sugar instead of the white sugar.

FRENCH ICE-CREAM

6 egg-yolks
5 cups medium cream

¾ cup sugar
Vanilla bean

Scald the cream with a piece of vanilla bean. Beat the egg-yolks, add the sugar and pour the cream slowly on the mixture, beating constantly. Cook in a double boiler until it thickens, watching it carefully. Cool and freeze.

CHOCOLATE PECAN CREAM

1 square chocolate
⅔ cup sugar
2 tablespoons boiling water
2 cups thin cream

1 cup pecan nut-meats
⅔ teaspoon vanilla
⅛ teaspoon salt

Melt the chocolate, add sugar, and cook with water until smooth and glossy. Add the cream slowly, then the salt, the pecan-meats crushed into small pieces, and the vanilla. Cool and freeze.

Serve with a topping of whipped cream and a few pecan-meats. Other nuts may be used instead of the pecans, if desired.

FRESH-FRUIT ICE-CREAM

Prepare fruit by sprinkling sugar over it. Let it stand one hour, press through a coarse sieve and stir into American ice-cream when the cream is frozen to a mush.

If seed fruits, such as currants, are used, strain through a fine sieve or a piece of cheese-cloth and use the juice only. The juice can be put into the freezer with the cream and not served until later, as in the case of the mashed fruits.

Grated pineapple wtih the addition of a little lemon-juice makes a particularly fine fruit cream.

PEACH ICE-CREAM

1 pint milk	2 egg-yolks
2 tablespoons flour	1 cup heavy cream
2 tablespoons water	2 cups peach-pulp and juice
1 cup sugar	

Make custard as directed for vanilla ice-cream. When cool, add the peach-pulp and juice, and freeze.

ICE-CREAM SANDWICHES

Devil's food, angel cake, sponge cake, butter cake, or éclair or cream-puff shells may be the foundation of many a delicious ice-cream sandwich. Between thin slices of any of the cakes, or between halves of pastry shells, place a serving of ice-cream of a flavor to blend well with the cake. Brick ice-cream, of course, is the easiest to cut. Cover with chocolate, butterscotch, marshmallow, or fruit sauce, either hot or cold, and top with nuts of various kinds, coconut, or pieces of fresh or canned fruit.

For example, between thin slices of gold or white cake place a serving of vanilla ice-cream and three or four tablespoons of crushed fresh strawberries. Over the whole pour plain marshmallow sauce or whipped cream and garnish with several tablespoons of crushed strawberries. Fill a cream-puff shell with peach ice-cream and pour over it a peach sirup, topped with whipped cream. Chocolate or vanilla ice-cream placed between layers of white cake or angel food is delicious covered with a thick fudge sauce.

MAPLE MOUSSE

1¼ cups maple sirup   2 tablespoons gelatin
½ cup sugar   ¼ cup cold water
5 cups cream

Combine maple sirup, sugar and one cup of cream and bring to a boil, stirring constantly. Add the gelatin softened in water and dissolved over heat. Strain, cool in ice-water until the mixture thickens, then add the remainder of the cream, whipped stiff. Place in a mold, pack in ice and salt and let stand for four hours.

GRAPE ICE

⅔ cup sugar   1½ cup water
1 cup grape-juice   2 tablespoons lemon-juice
¼ cup orange-juice

Boil the sugar and water together for five minutes. Mix all the ingredients together, strain and freeze.

PINEAPPLE SHERBET

1 quart water   2 cups shredded pineapple,
2 cups sugar   fresh or canned
1 lemon   2 egg-whites

Boil water and sugar together for five minutes. Chop pineapple (it may be put through a food-chopper if a pan is put below to catch the juice), scald it in the boiling sirup, and rub through a sieve. Cool, add lemon-juice and freeze to a mush. Add the beaten whites of the eggs and continue freezing.

CIDER FRAPPÉ

1½ cups sugar   2 cups orange-juice
1 pint water   ½ cup lemon-juice
1 quart sweet cider

Boil sugar and water together for five minutes. Add cider and fruit-juices. Cool, strain and freeze to a mush.

CRANBERRY FRAPPÉ

1 quart cranberries   2 cups sugar
1 pint water   Juice of 2 lemons

Cook the cranberries and water together for ten minutes, then force through a sieve. Add the sugar and the juice of the lemons, cool and freeze to a mush.

MARSHMALLOW SAUCE

¾ cup sugar
¼ cup milk

½ pound marshmallows
2 tablespoons water

Boil the sugar and milk until the sirup threads. When almost cold, beat until thick and white. Set in boiling water and stir until thin enough to pour. Stir the marshmallows with the water in a double boiler until smooth. Pour the sirup over the melted marshmallows and beat together. Keep warm, but not hot.

HOT FUDGE CHOCOLATE SAUCE

1 cup sugar
½ cup water
½ teaspoon vanilla

1 square chocolate
1 tablespoon butter

Mix together the sugar, water and grated chocolate. Boil for five minutes. Cool slightly and add the butter and vanilla.

STRAWBERRY OR RASPBERRY SAUCE

¼ cup butter or butter substitute
1 cup powdered sugar

1 egg-white
1 cup strawberries or raspberries

Cream the butter or butter substitute, add the sugar gradually, the stiffly beaten egg-whites, and the mashed berries. Beat until well mixed and foamy. A little lemon-juice will improve the flavor.

PASTRY

APPLE PIE

4 to 6 tart apples
¼ cup water
1 egg-yolk
1 cup sugar

1 tablespoon butter
1 teaspoon nutmeg
Powdered sugar

Line a pie-pan with plain crust and fill with thinly sliced apples. Add the water and cover with a top crust, making it a little richer than the under one. This is easily done by rolling in bits of fat and folding the paste several times. Cut a few slits in the center of the top crust to allow steam to escape while cooking. Brush with beaten yolk of egg. When baked, and while still hot, remove the top crust carefully sprinkle sugar over the cooked apple and dot with butter or butter substitute. Replace the top crust and dust with powdered sugar. This is an old-fashioned method. Ingredients given make one pie.

DEEP-DISH APPLE PIE (ENGLISH)

4 to 6 tart apples
1 cup sugar
1 teaspoon cinnamon

1 teaspoon butter
1 cup hard sauce

Invert a heavy china cup in the center of a baking-dish. Fill the dish full of apples, pared, cored and cut in slices. Cover the dish with plain paste rolled a little thicker than usual, and slashed to allow the steam to escape. Bake for three-quarters of an hour, then remove from oven, and, with a knife, carefully pry up the crust and season with sugar, cinnamon and butter. When serving, slip the knife under the cup to allow the confined juice to mix with the apple. Serve the pie hot with a hard sauce.

MOCK CHERRY PIE

1 cup cranberries
½ cup seeded raisins
¾ cup sugar

1 tablespoon flour
1 teaspoon almond extract
1 teaspoon butter

Deep dish apple pie is rich and juicy and delicious. The directions for making it are given on page 174.

Cranberry pie is usually baked in a single shell with a lattice work of piecrust over the top.

Raisins and dried peaches, lemon juice and sugar, make the
filling of the pie above.

A lemon filling, a baked shell and a topping of meringue make
lemon meringue pie. See page 178.

Line a pie-pan with crust. Fill with cranberries, washed and cut in halves, mixed with chopped raisins. Sprinkle with mixture of sugar and flour, add almond extract, and dot with butter. Cover with a second crust, and bake.

RHUBARB MERINGUE PIE

5 to 8 stalks rhubarb
Flour
1 cup sugar
¼ cup water

2 egg-whites
1 tablespoon sugar for meringue

Line a pie-pan with plain paste. Cut into pieces sufficient rhubarb to fill the pan, and sprinkle with flour until each piece is quite white. Place the rhubarb in the pie-pan, adding one cup of sugar and a very little water. Bake slowly, and when done spread over the top the stiffly beaten whites of the eggs into which has been folded one tablespoon of sugar. Return to oven and brown lightly.

PRUNE PIE

1 cup cooked and pitted prunes
1 lemon, juice and grated rind
1 cup water or juice

1 tablespoon flour
½ cup sugar
2 tablespoons butter

Cook the prunes with the other ingredients until slightly thickened. Add a little cinnamon or nutmeg, if desired. Bake between two crusts. Shredded coconut may be added to the filling, for variation. Prune pie is delicious served with ice-cream or whipped cream. This amount makes a small pie.

BUTTERSCOTCH PIE

1½ cup milk
1 cup brown sugar
3 tablespoons corn-starch

2 eggs
2 tablespoons butter
2 tablespoons powdered sugar

Heat one cup of milk and the sugar until the sugar is free from lumps. Mix the corn-starch, one-half cup milk and egg-yolks and add to the hot mixture slowly. Cook in a double boiler until thick, stirring constantly, then for ten minutes longer. Add butter. When cool, pour into a baked shell. Cover with a meringue made from the stiffly beaten egg-whites and the powdered sugar. Brown in the oven.

As an attractive variation, cover the top of the pie with halves of marshmallows and brown in the oven. In this case, one whole egg instead of two yolks may be used in the filling.

CREAM PIE AND ITS VARIATIONS

1 cup milk
1 tablespoon corn-starch
¼ cup sugar

Few grains of salt
2 egg-yolks or 1 whole egg
1 teaspoon vanilla

Scald the milk. Mix the corn-starch, sugar and salt, and add hot milk slowly. Cook twenty minutes over hot water. Beat the egg-yolks and add slowly, stirring rapidly. Cool and add vanilla. Put into a baked crust. Vary in any of the following ways:

Banana or orange pie—Slice fruit into baked crust and cover with custard filling. Cover top with meringue made from egg-whites.

Chocolate pie—Use only seven-eighths tablespoon corn-starch. Add two squares of grated chocolate just before removing custard from the stove. Beat well. Cover with meringue.

Coconut pie—Add two tablespoons shredded coconut to the meringue made from the egg-whites.

Nut pie—Stir one cup of chopped nuts into the filling and sprinkle the top with a few. Raisins and nuts may be used together.

Spice pie—Add two teaspoons each of ground cloves and cinnamon to the cooked filling.

Date pie—Add one cup of chopped dates. Cover with meringue.

LEMON PIE

1½ tablespoons corn-starch
1 cup water
1 tablespoon butter
1 cup sugar

1 lemon
1 egg-white
1 to 3 tablespoons sugar

Mix the corn-starch in a little of the cold water and bring the rest of the water to the boiling-point. Add the moistened corn-starch and cook until transparent. Add the butter, sugar, lemon-juice and grated rind and set aside to cool. Beat the mixture well and turn into a baked crust. Make a meringue with the stiffly beaten white of egg and sugar. Brown the meringue and serve the pie cold.

PUMPKIN PIE

1½ cups prepared pumpkin	1 teaspoon salt
⅔ cup brown sugar	2 eggs
1 teaspoon cinnamon	2 cups milk
½ teaspoon ginger	

Steam and strain fresh pumpkin or bake it and put it through a
sieve. Canned pumpkin is ready to use. Add remaining ingredients in the order given. Turn into a crust-lined pan and
bake. Use a rather high temperature at first, to cook the bottom
and sides of crust. Reduce the temperature and continue cooking
until a silver knife inserted in the center will come out clean. Do
not let the pie boil, as that will make it watery.

Nut-meats (one-half cup) are a delicious addition. Whipped
cream is also very good with pumpkin pie.

APPLE TARTS

5 apples	¾ cup granulated sugar
½ cup cold water	2 tablespoons butter
3 eggs	2 tablespoons powdered sugar
1 lemon	

Pare, core and cut up tart apples and cook them in the water
until soft, stewing them very slowly. Beat this sauce smooth,
partly cool, then add beaten egg-yolks, lemon-juice and grated
rind and the granulated sugar, increasing the amount of sugar,
if desired. Line patty-pans with paste, fill them with the mixture, dot with butter and bake in a very hot oven. Beat the
whites of the eggs stiff, add the powdered sugar, spread on top
of the tarts and return to the oven to brown. This amount makes
six to eight tarts.

BANANA ROLL

Peel bananas and cut in halves crosswise. Roll puff or flaky
paste one-eighth of an inch thick. Cut into pieces. Dip each
piece in ice-water and wrap around a half banana. Place on a
baking-sheet and bake in a moderate oven. Serve with a sauce
made by crushing strawberries with sugar.

MAMMY'S FRIED PIES

Stew dried apples, peaches or apricots. Drain off all juice,
mash well and sweeten. Roll pie-crust one-eighth inch thick and

cut circles three inches in diameter. On one of the circles place a spoonful of the filling, having a clear margin of the pie-crust. Moisten this edge all around, place another circle on top and press the edges firmly together. Fry in deep fat like doughnuts or sauté with a little fat in a hot frying-pan, turning the pie so that it will brown on both sides. These are good with fillings of mince meat or cooked rice.

PEANUT STRIPS

Peanut butter
Lemon-juice

Egg-white
Chopped peanuts

Roll paste very thin. Place on inverted baking-tin. Brush half with peanut butter thinned with lemon-juice. Cover with the other half and with a sharp knife mark in strips four inches long and one inch wide. Set in a quick oven. When baked, brush with white of egg diluted with one teaspoon of cold water and sprinkle with finely chopped peanuts. Return to the oven for about three minutes, until the nuts are slightly crisped, then cut apart. These are excellent with coffee or afternoon tea.

RASPBERRY TURNOVERS

Cut circles of puff or flaky paste three inches in diameter, having the paste not more than one-eighth of an inch thick. Moisten half the edge of the circle with cold water and in the center lay a teaspoon of thick raspberry preserve. Fold one half of the circle over the other, making edges meet. Press closely and mark with a fork dipped in flour. Brush with beaten egg, prick, and chill before placing in the oven. Dust with granulated sugar before serving. If desired, decorate the top of each with a single preserved berry or a candied cherry. Other fruit may be used in the same way.

Pastry shells are first baked crispy brown and then filled; turnovers, page 180, are filled beforehand.

A pastry shell, full of luscious cherries, served on a glass plate,
is an alluring looking dessert.

A cup or glass of tea is a delicious hot or cold beverage, and delightfully refreshing.

For hot weather there is no cold drink more tempting or healthful than a mixed fruit punch. See page 183.

BEVERAGES

HOSTESS COCOA

Mix 5 tablespoons cocoa, few grains of salt, 3 tablespoons sugar and 1 cup cold water. Simmer slowly for ten minutes. Add to 3 cups scalded milk or evaporated milk (diluted) and cook 25 to 30 minutes in doube boiler. Add 2 teaspoons vanilla, beat thoroughly with egg beater and serve with sweetened and flavored ice cream. For a most delicious variation, ¼ cup strong coffee may be added with the scalded milk and 2 tablespoons sherry flavoring added with the vanilla.

CHOCOLATE

Cook 2 squares chocolate, 3 tablespoons sugar, 1/16 teaspoon salt and ¼ cup boiling water until very smooth, stirring constantly. Stir in 1 teaspoon cornstarch mixed with 2 tablespoons of cold milk. Add this chocolate mixture gradually to 4 cups scalded milk or evaporated milk (diluted) and cook 15 minutes in double boiler. Add 2 teaspoons vanilla, beat well with an egg beater until foamy and serve with whipped cream.

FROSTED MOCHA CHOCOLATE

Combine 4 cups chocolate in which a stick of cinnamon has been cooked with 1 cup strong coffee, using 1½ cups sugar in all. Serve frappéd or as a granite, with or without whipped cream.

LEMON FROST

Fill a tall glass one-fourth full of cracked ice, fill three-fourths full of lemonade and frost the top with a spoonful of stiffly beaten egg-white sweetened slightly and flavored with lemon-juice.

GINGER-ALE PUNCH

Juice of 4 lemons
1 pint grape juice

Sugar or sirup to taste
1 quart ginger ale

Mix fruit-juices and sugar or sirup. Just before serving, add ginger ale.

CHILLED GRAPE-JUICE

Wash purple grapes and boil under skin, pulp and seeds separate. Press through jelly-bag and to every pint of juice add one-half cup of sugar. Boil for twenty minutes, chill and serve with chipped ice.

GRAPE-JUICE HIGH BALL

Use Niagara grapes. Proceed as for recipe for chilled grape-juice. Serve in tall glasses half filled with shaved ice and add an equal quantity of charged water. Lemon is an attractive addition.

QUAKER DRINK

3 sprigs of mint	Juice of 3 oranges
3 cups tea infusion	½ teaspoon powdered ginger
Juice of 3 lemons	2 cups cold water

Bruise mint in a pitcher and pour the tea over the fruit-juice, ginger mixed with two tablespoons hot water and the cold water. Chill and serve.

ORANGE LILY

½ cup white grape-juice	2 tablespoons orange-juice
1 teaspoon sugar	

Fill glass half full of shaved ice. Add grape-juice, orange-juice and sugar and fill with chilled water. Serve with two straws thrust through a thin slice of orange.

VERANDA PUNCH

Juice of 3 lemons	1 cup tea infusion
Juice of 2 oranges	1 pint ginger ale
½ cup sugar sirup	1 pint charged water

Mix fruit-juice and sugar sirup. Add the hot tea. Cool, and, when ready to serve, add ginger ale and charged water. Thin slices of lemon and orange may be used for a garnish.

CASSEROLE AND OVEN COOKERY

The expression "en casserole" is sometimes misunderstood because the word "casserole" is used in two quite different ways by writers on domestic subects. Properly speaking, a casserole is the coarse clay saucepan, so common in France, in which meats and vegetables are not only cooked but served on the table. In its other usage the word is applied to a case or mold of potato, rice or fried bread, inside of which is placed some preparation of meat or vegetables. The word in this case really signifies a border or croustade. Directions for using this second form of casserole will be found in the chapter on entrées.

VARIETIES OF CASSEROLES

Casseroles of different sizes, shapes and materials, are convenient additions to the cooking equipment, and should be chosen with consideration for the needs of the family. They come in many sizes from the individual ramekin up to one that will hold two chickens. They may be had in various shapes—oval and round, shallow and deep. They are made in a variety of materials—glass, vitrified china, earthenware, iron and aluminum—and in a color-range that allows one to choose according to personal preference—brown, yellow, green, blue and mixtures.

CARE OF CASSEROLES

Casseroles will last indefinitely if properly treated. It is wise to avoid a sudden and great change in temperature, such as occurs when a casserole is taken from a hot oven and placed in a wet sink. It is not advisable to set a glass or earthenware casserole over a high flame without an asbestos mat under it. A new casserole may be tempered and made more tough by pouring cold water into and about it, and bringing it gradually to the boiling-point.

ADVANTAGES OF COOKING IN A CASSEROLE

The Casserole Saves Dish-Washing, because it makes it possible to bring food to the table in the dish in which it was cooked. Frequently, also, it contains a "one-dish meal" which eliminates all but the one cooking dish.

The Casserole Makes it Possible to Use Left-Overs in attractive, palatable combinations, to cook tough meats tender, and to prepare vegetables in an almost unlimited variety of ways. Any vegetable may be boiled, steamed, baked, scalloped or creamed, and cabbage, cucumbers, eggplant, onions, peppers, potatoes or tomatoes may be stuffed and cooked in the casserole.

Food Cooked in This Way Needs Little Watching, it may be kept warm and still attractive if the meal is delayed, and there is no loss of vegetable or meat juices. These juices contain a valuable part of the food which is often thrown away, especially in the case of vegetables that are boiled.

A Whole Meal May Be Cooking in the Oven in the casserole while the oven is being used for some other purpose, such as baking cookies. The cover of the casserole should fit well into the dish, so that it is practically airtight, a fact that should be borne in mind when the casserole is purchased. If the oven must be kept very hot for something else, set the casserole in a pan of water so that the food within will simmer, not boil. As the water becomes hot, take out part of it and add cool water to keep it at the desired temperature.

CHICKEN EN CASSEROLE

1 chicken	12 potato balls
Butter, salad oil, or other fat	1 carrot, sliced
1 pint rich brown stock	6 small onions
12 button mushrooms	Salt, pepper, paprika

Wash the chicken and cut it up. Sauté the pieces in a little fat until well browned on all sides. Place in a greased casserole, add brown stock, cover and cook in a slow to moderate oven (350° F.) for an hour.

When the chicken has been cooking for an hour, sauté the carrot slices, the potato balls, the onions and the mushrooms in a little fat, stirring them lightly around until they are well browned. Put these with the chicken in the casserole, season with salt, pepper and paprika, add more salt if needed, cover

and cook for three-fourths of an hour, then remove the cover
and allow the chicken to brown before serving.

PIGEONS EN CASSEROLE

Pigeons or squabs
Bacon
3 tablespoons butter or other
fat

1 Spanish onion
Veal broth or white stock
Vegetables, as desired
Flour

Clean and wash young pigeons and tie a strip of bacon around
each one, or lard the breasts if preferred. Place the butter or
other fat in a casserole, slice a mild, Spanish onion over the fat,
set the pigeons on the onion in the casserole, cover the casserole
and set on the stove over a low heat with an asbestos mat under
the casserole to protect it from direct heat and to insure slow
cooking. Cook on top of the stove for fifteen minutes. Add
enough veal broth or white stock to half cover the pigeons and
set in the oven (350° F.) to cook until tender (2-2½ hrs.).
When nearly done, vegetables may be added. At serving-time
thicken the liquor in the casserole by stirring into it flour mixed
smooth in a little water, allowing one tablespoon of flour for
each cup of liquid.

STEAK EN CASSEROLE

3 tablespoons butter or
other fat
3 tablespoons flour
2 cups stock
Salt
Parsley

Pepper
Turnip balls
Carrot balls
Potato balls
Small onions
2 pounds of 1½-inch steak

Make a brown sauce of the fat, flour, stock and seasoning.
Add balls of turnip, carrot, potato and onions, which have
been previously cooked in a little brown stock until tender.
For each person, allow a half-dozen little balls of each of these
vegetables and two small onions. Keep this sauce hot while
you pan-broil the steak until about half done, then transfer
steak to heated casserole, pour vegetables and sauce over steak,
cover, and place in oven (350° F.) until steak is sufficiently
cooked. When ready to serve, sprinkle the steak with finely
chopped parsley.

CHOPPED BEEF EN CASSEROLE

2 pounds clod of beef   Boiled beets
⅔ cup tomato catchup   Salt
⅛ teaspoon tabasco sauce

Mix chopped beef with tomato catchup. Add tabasco sauce, using more if desired. Season well with salt. Place in casserole and bake (350° F.) slowly two to two and one-half hours, basting frequently with water and tabasco or Worcestershire sauce. A few strips of bacon across the top will add to the richness, and improve the flavor. Garnish with quartered beets.

TAMALE PIE EN CASSEROLE

1 cup yellow corn-meal   2 cups chopped beef
6 cups boiling water   2 cups tomatoes
1 teaspoon salt   2 pimientos
1 medium-sized onion   Cayenne
2 tablespoons fat

Cook corn-meal, water, and salt, as for mush, for about thirty minutes. Chop onion and fry in fat till brown. Add meat and fry until red color disappears. Add tomatoes, pimientos, and cayenne. Line oiled casserole with mush, put meat mixture in center, cover with mush, and bake in a moderate oven (350° F.; 2-2½ hrs.).

TURBANS OF FISH EN CASSEROLE

Prepare slices of halibut or other fish about the size of one's hand, with all bone and skin removed and sufficiently thin to roll easily. Trim all to uniform size, dip each in melted butter or other fat, squeeze over them lemon-juice and onion-juice, and sprinkle with salt. Beginning at the widest end, roll the slice of fish and secure with two toothpicks. Set the turban in a greased and heated casserole and pour in a little stock made by simmering the bones and trimmings of the fish in a little water, together with a few slices each of carrot and onion. Cook in a moderate oven (350° F.) basting occasionally. When done, drain off the liquid and thicken it with flour mixed with cold water. Return to the casserole, and reheat.

HUNGARIAN GOULASH EN CASSEROLE

4 onions
2 pounds veal
Bacon fat
1½ pints brown stock
Pepper
1 pint potato balls

12 small onions
1 cup carrot slices
1 cup turnip slices
Salt
Paprika

Slice the onion and cut the raw veal in cubes. Cook together in a little bacon fat, until brown. Transfer to casserole, pour over it the brown stock and season with pepper and paprika. Place in moderate oven (350° F.). Add more fat to that in the frying-pan and brown in this the potato balls, small onions, and slices of carrot and turnip. Add the vegetables and salt to the casserole when the meat is partly cooked. Finish the cooking, adding more stock if necessary. This dish should cook two hours. If the broth is too thin when ready to serve, thicken slightly with browned flour rubbed smooth in water.

LAMB EN CASSEROLE

6 slices of lamb
2 tablespoons melted butter or
    other fat
2 cups brown stock

1 pint vegetable balls
12 small onions
Seasoning

Cut thick slices from a leg of lamb and sear, browning both sides. Brush with melted fat and place in casserole with one-half to one cup of brown stock. Cook on top of the stove or in a moderate oven (350° F.) until tender, then add potato balls, carrot balls and onions, which have been previously cooked. Add more brown stock, salt, pepper and paprika.

PORK CHOPS EN CASSEROLE

6 pork chops
6 sweet potatoes
Salt and pepper

½ cup brown sugar
1 to 2 cups milk

Place a layer of sweet potatoes, sliced crosswise, in a greased casserole, dust with salt, pepper, and a little brown sugar; continue the layers until the casserole is about two-thirds full. Heat the milk and pour it over the potatoes; it should just cover them. Place the pork chops on top of the potatoes, cover and bake (at 350° F.) for an hour, then remove the cover and season with salt and pepper. Leave the cover off and cook until the chops are tender and nicely browned on top.

Four tart apples, pared, cored and cut in eighths, used in place of the sweet potatoes, make an excellent casserole dish with pork chops.

CALF'S LIVER EN CASSEROLE

1 calf's liver
6 slices bacon
1 cup button mushrooms

3 cups potato balls
1 pint brown stock

Wash a calf's liver thoroughly and wipe dry. Fry some bacon in a pan, remove, place the liver in the bacon fat, and sear each side thoroughly. Transfer to a casserole, add slices of bacon, brown stock, and sautéd mushrooms. Cook for one hour and a half in the oven (350° F.) adding more stock if necessary. Just before serving add potato balls which have been fried in deep fat (395° F.) and drained.

CASSEROLE OF RICE AND LIVER

1 cup rice
1 quart water
2 tablespoons butter or other
    fat
1 pound lamb's or calf's liver
2 cups stock

1 teaspoon caramel
2 tablespoons browned flour
2 tablespoons fat
Crumbs
Salt and pepper

Boil the rice in the water and mash smooth with the fat. Season with salt and pepper to taste. Line a well-greased casserole with the mixture, pressing the paste firmly against bottom and sides, and leaving a large hollow in the center. Set in a cold place until firm. Meanwhile boil the liver, drain, chop fine and season with salt. Heat the soup stock, seasoned with caramel. Make a brown sauce with the fat, browned flour and soup stock, and add the minced liver. Fill the hollow in the center of the rice with the liver mixture, sprinkle with crumbs and brown in the oven.

RICE EN CASSEROLE

2 cups chopped cold meat
3 eggs
⅓ cup milk
2 cups boiled rice
Celery-salt

2 tablespoons butter or other fat
2 tablespoons tomato catchup
Salt

Season the meat and pile it in the center of an oiled casserole. Mix the eggs, milk, rice, fat and seasonings. Pour over the meat, cover, and bake (350° F.) for twenty minutes.

SPANISH RICE

¾ cup rice
2 tablespoons fat
5 cups water
2 onions
2 cups tomatoes

½ cup chopped green pepper or pimientos
Salt
Pepper
Paprika

Fry the rice in the fat until brown, then add water and boil until soft. Drain. Sauté the onions in a little fat; mix with tomatoes and chopped peppers or pimientos, and add to the rice. Add seasoning, and place in a greased casserole. Bake (350° F.) for thirty minutes.

RICE A LA CREOLE

1 cup chopped boiled or raw ham
1 onion
1 cup boiled rice
1 can tomatoes

2 cups fine soft crumbs
2 tablespoons butter or other fat
Celery-salt
Pepper and salt

Mix ingredients in the order given. Bake in a greased casserole for one-half hour (350° F.). This dish makes a good one-dish meal.

SPAGHETTI, SPANISH MICHEL

2 cups spaghetti
1 quart tomatoes, fresh or canned
½ cup boiled ham

1 onion
1 green pepper
¼ teaspoon pepper
½ teaspoon salt

Break the spaghetti into inch pieces. Cook in one quart boiling water until tender, add the tomatoes, and cook fifteen minutes longer. Remove the fat from the ham and try it out, Dice onions and green pepper, and fry slowly in this fat until tender. Chop the ham and add it with the onion, green pepper and seasoning to the spaghetti and tomatoes. Put in casserole and bake fifteen minutes in a moderate oven (350°-400° F.).

SCALLOPED HAM AND POTATOES

6 potatoes
1 pound raw smoked ham
3 cups milk (or more)

1 green pepper (may be omitted)
Flour

Cover the bottom of an oiled baking-dish with sliced, raw potatoes. Sprinkle with flour add inch-square pieces of ham. Repeat until the dish is full. Pour in as much milk as the dish will hold. Bake (350°-400° F.) until the potatoes are tender (1-1½ hrs.). Chopped green pepper adds to the flavor.

SUMMER CASSEROLE

6 hard-cooked eggs
3 ripe tomatoes
3 tablespoons butter or other fat
3 tablespoons flour

2 teaspoons salt
1½ cups milk
½ cup grated cheese
Buttered crumbs

Cut hard-cooked eggs in half and arrange around the edge of a greased casserole or baking-dish. Slice peeled ripe tomatoes in the center of the dish. Make a white sauce of the milk, fat and flour. Add cheese, and stir over a very low fire until the cheese is well mixed and smooth. Pour over tomatoes and eggs. Cover with crumbs and bake twenty minutes in a moderate oven (350°-400° F.).

The centers of the tomatoes may be scooped out, and a whole egg placed in each, if desired.

BANANAS EN CASSEROLE

6 small bananas
1 glass currant or grape jelly

1 cup boiling water
1 lemon

Peel the bananas. Remove the coarse threads and divide in quarters, cutting first crosswise and then lengthwise. Place in a greased casserole and pour over them a sauce made by melting the currant or grape jelly in the boiling water, and mixing with

Above, light and well seasoned, with tops slightly browned, are potatoes on the half shell, page 108.

The succulent looking discs are hot broiled tomatoes, page 112, with melted butter as a sauce.

The vegetable plate, an appetizing arrangement of vegetables, makes an excellent luncheon, page 84.

Interesting to look at and delicious to taste, the French artichoke, page 99, may be served hot or cold.

it the juice of a lemon. Cover the casserole and bake in a hot oven (400°-450° F.) until the bananas are tender. The cover may be removed at the last moment and the bananas sprinkled with granulated sugar and allowed to brown slightly. Serve as an entrée with game, mutton, or beef.

AU GRATIN DISHES EN CASSEROLE

Au gratin dishes, many of which are given in this book, are particularly adapted to the casserole. The mixtures of chicken, sweetbreads, fish, macaroni and vegetables may be entirely prepared, then placed in the casserole, topped with buttered crumbs, and cheese and placed in a hot oven (400°-450° F.) to brown.

COOKING FOR TWO

The problem here is really more one of planning and marketing than of actual cooking. No roast leg of lamb or baked ham of course, no standing rib roast of beef, not often a whole watermelon. But it is possible to buy cuts of meat and to plan the other marketing so that to all intents and purposes these favorites may form part of the menu even for the smallest family. Morover, many dishes which are too expensive to be served to a large and hungry family are often possible for a family of two.

COOKING EQUIPMENT FOR TWO

It is impossible to cook small quantities satisfactorily in large dishes; so the first thing to do is to buy dishes and utensils of the right size. The following list is given as a suggestion.

A small casserole or a large ramekin for soufflés and casserole dishes, to be used either for the meat course or for baked puddings.

Individual ramekins and custard cups.

A small frying-pan for cooking eggs, bacon, etc.

A small baking-pan for roasting meat.

Small saucepans and kettles for vegetables and other boiled foods. The saucepans that fit together, two or three on a single burner, are especially good for the small family.

A deep pot of small diameter for deep fat frying and a wire strainer that will fit down inside it to be used as a frying basket.

A double boiler holding one quart.

Muffin pans in sets of six.

Layer cake and pie pans five or six inches in diameter.

A small square or oblong shallow pan for baking sheets of cake, ginger-bread, etc.

A small loaf pan for breads, loaf cakes and meat loaves.

A set of skewers for serving "en brochette."

A cup sized egg beater.

Small bowls.

An ice cream freezer either of the crank or vacuum type, holding from one pint to one quart.

The small ovens for use on top of the stove are very convenient for baking two or three potatoes or apples or a small dish of rice pudding, custard and similar desserts.

HOW TO MODIFY RECIPES

Recipes in the Delineator Cook Book are standardized for six persons. All but a few can be cut down to one-half or one-third and made exactly as though the entire quantity were being used. It is usually better to cut the recipe in half rather than in thirds, however, since it is hard to handle the smaller amounts and there is proportionately a greater waste of food adhering to the dishes, pans and spoons.

In Cooking Over Direct Fire or in the oven, the loss of moisture will be comparatively larger than in the larger quantity recipe, so a little more liquid may be used. This is true particularly in recipes that use cream sauces and in meat casseroles.

Recipes Including Eggs are more easily made if they can be divided to the one or two egg quantity. If less than one egg has to be used, there are two ways of doing it: Either use a very small egg or beat the egg slightly and divide it, keeping the unused portion for some other dish. It might be well to say, however, that a little more egg than the recipe calls for will not generally do any harm. So if you are not considering economy you will be safe in using a whole egg even though the rest of the ingredients are cut down.

With Yeast Dough it is advisable to use a larger quantity of yeast, proportionately, than would be used in the full recipe. For instance, if the recipe calls for one yeast cake, and you are cutting it down to one-third or one-half, it will be wise to use the whole yeast cake, or the greater part of it, in order to hasten the process. Those recipes which demand no kneading are easier than the kneaded ones to handle in small quantities.

For Soups, allow from one-half cup to one cup for each person, the amount depending upon the kind of soup you are making and whether you are serving it in cups or plates.

For Desserts, allow from one-half cup to three-quarters cup for each serving.

Of Creamed Dishes, vegetables, etc., about two-thirds cup is served, but an allowance for a second portion should be made.

TO USE ONE RECIPE IN DIFFERENT WAYS

Often a full recipe can be made and used in different ways for several occasions.

The Recipe for Creamed Chicken, for instance, will provide enough for an au gratin oven dish.

A Rich Baking Powder Biscuit Dough will make shortcakes for one meal, toasted biscuits for another, and, if baked in a sheet and covered with cinnamon and sugar, coffee-cake for a third.

Pie Dough will make pies, tart shells for meat or dessert, cheese strips for soup or salad, and tiny jam turnovers for afternoon tea.

Cake Batter may be baked as loaves, layers, sheets or cup cakes, as cottage pudding, to be served hot with a sauce, or as a ring in which to serve fruit, jelly or a creamed dessert. A fruit cake mixture may be baked as fruit cake or steamed in small molds and served hot with sauce.

HOW TO USE LEFT-OVERS

The secret of success in cooking for two depends to a great extent for its solution upon the ability to use left-overs attractively at successive meals. In using this surplus food, it is important to supply whatever is lacking. If it is dry it needs to be moistened; if it is hard it needs to be softened; if it is not of any particular flavor it needs to be well seasoned or mixed with something that will give it a distinctive and appetizing taste.

Sometimes It Is Well to Keep Your Left-Overs Uncooked. For instance, if you have a steak that is too large for one meal, because in order to have it appetizing you had to have it cut fairly thick, cut out the heart or tenderloin and broil it, keeping the rest for a fresh-meat casserole the next day.

Any Small Pieces of Uncooked Meat may be made attractive by broiling on the skewer or preparing as a mixed grill or a mixed fried dish. For any of these there need be only a few small pieces of meat with accessories such as half a dozen mushrooms, a few slices of potato, an onion or two, small cubes of egg-plant or turnip or other vegetables, a few curls of bacon or a tiny sausage or two. To cook "en brochette" dip the small pieces of meat and vegetable in melted butter and impale them on the skewer. Bacon and sausage of course need no butter.

Put the skewer on the broiling rack and broil, turning occasionally. For a mixed grill, any meat or vegetable that can be put under the broiler may be used. Slices of tomato, eggplant and pineapple give interesting variety.

MEATS FOR TWO

The following types of meat dishes are as easily served to two as to six:

Hamburg balls or steak	Chop suey
Lamb, mutton, veal or pork chops	Sausages
	Scrapple
Liver	Dried beef
Kidneys	Sliced ham
Sweetbreads	Bacon
Ox tails	Salt pork

Roasts—Instead of a large roast of beef, buy a thick steak, roll, tie and roast it in a very hot oven (450°-500° F.) for a short time. If even this is too large a roast, cut out the heart for roasting and keep the rest for a casserole dish.

For Lamb, Mutton and Veal Roasts, buy loin chops—as many as you require. Have the bones separated at the joints but do not have the meat cut through. Cook as a standing roast.

For Baked Ham, buy a one-inch thick slice of raw ham. Brown it on both sides in the frying-pan, then cover it with mustard, flour and sugar and stuff the top with cloves. Add a little water and cook, covered, in a moderate oven (350° F.) for an hour.

In Place of Stuffed Shoulder of Lamb, mutton or veal, buy a slice of the meat and spread it with any desired stuffing. Roll, with the stuffing inside. This may be browned first and then baked, or may be put immediately into the oven.

For Pot Roasts a one-pound or two-pound piece will be quite as satisfactory as a larger one, though it may require a little more watching while it is cooking.

Poultry—A whole turkey, of course, is out of the question, but poultry may be enjoyed in the shape of a broiling chicken or guinea chick, or squab and the smaller game birds, quail and grouse. These can be broiled, fried or baked. The pigeon is nice in a pie.

FISH

Whole Fish that will serve six or more persons are not a wise purchase for the small family. Either buy small fish, such as smelts, perch and butterfish, or a steak or fillet from one of the large fish—halibut, cod, haddock, salmon and the like.

Shell Fish are particularly well suited to the needs of the small family. It is possible to buy just the right amount of clams, oysters, shrimps, hard and soft-shelled crabs, and sometimes a lobster just large enough for two is procurable. Shad roe and frogs' legs are luxuries that are more often possible for the small family than for the large family.

VEGETABLES

The Large Vegetables will give left-overs that can be used in many ways. A small cabbage makes one nice salad, and, a few days later, one cooked dish. Winter squash can be used up in pies and custards. An egg-plant will give one-half for stuffing and baking and several slices for frying, with some, perhaps left to cook in Oriental style. Left-over cooked cauliflower may be served cold as a salad, or scalloped.

The Smaller Vegetables, fresh peas, beans, carrots, beets, potatoes, etc., can be bought and cooked in exactly the quantity required, though, as all of these are good for use in salads, it is generally wise to cook a little more than you need for one meal.

Spaghetti, Macaroni and Noodles are often served as a vegetable. These, of course, are easily managed if there are cooking utensils of the right size.

SOUPS

Any Creamed Vegetable Soup can be made in a pint quantity.

A Quart of Meat Stock can be made from the bones and trimmings of meat purchased for other cooking, and whatever is not needed for soup can be made into gravies and sauces for following days. A thickened meat stock containing small pieces of meat and plenty of diced vegetables makes a substantial dish.

BREADS

One Loaf of Yeast Bread can be made at a time, and quickly, if the proportion of yeast is increased.

Any Baking Powder Mixture can be mixed in the desired quantity, and almost any kind of loaf can be made with it— white, whole wheat, graham, oatmeal, bran, nut, raisin, etc. Baked in a small pan, these loaves will be used up before they are dry.

Biscuits and Muffins are the ideal home made bread for the small family.

Pancakes and Waffles are always possible, and may be served as breakfast or luncheon breads, as accompaniments to meat or chicken, or as a dessert, with fruit, honey, maple sirup or a sauce. With a table griddle or iron they can be cooked in the dining-room and served piping hot.

CAKES

A Layer or Loaf Cake which can be consumed in one or two meals can be baked in small pans. Half of an average recipe will make two of these small layers as well as several cup cakes or a sheet which can be cut into squares and frosted or not as desired.

If Rolled Cookies Are Too Much Trouble, use any recipe for drop cookies. These can be flattened out with a knife and made as thin as you wish.

DESSERTS

Puddings—With individual custard cups or ramekins or with one large enough to serve two, practically any baked pudding is possible, and with these same molds, custards or any of the cold puddings are easily molded. The recipes need no change other than cutting them to the desired quantity. It is easy to make one cup of custard or gelatin as it is to make a quart.

Most steamed puddings improve with keeping, so it is quite possible to make an entire recipe, steam it in small molds, and keep the extra ones for future need. They can be reheated in the top of a double boiler or in a pan, surrounded by water, in the oven. For strawberry shortcake of the old fashioned variety, cut the crust with a biscuit cutter and make individual shortcakes. For a sweet shortcake, bake the batter in muffin

pans.   Cottage pudding, soufflés, and similar desserts may be
baked in custard cups or ramekins and either turned out or
served in the dish with or without sauce.

Pies—A small sized pan will make as good a pie as a large
one.   If an extra shell is baked at the same time as a two-crust
pie, it can be kept for several days, then reheated to freshen it
and filled with a custard, cream or lemon filling.   Individual
tart shells made with the muffin tins, or turnovers just large
enough to serve one person make a variation in form.

FRUITS

These offer little difficulty, since most of them come in individual portions.   If you feel impelled to buy the large fruits,
such as watermelon, honeydew and cassaba melons, and pineapple, serve them in different ways so that they do not become
tiresome before they are eaten up.   From the pineapple make
a fruit cup, a salad, an open tart, frosting for cake or a delicous
sherbert or ice cream.   After the first slices of melon have been
used, cut balls and allow them to stand in fruit juice.   Serve,
chilled, as a fruit cup.   Watermelon can be used for a cooling
sherbet or frappé and the other melons make interesting fruit
salads.

NUTS

These should not be forgotten in planning meals for two.
Chestnuts, for example, make a delicious vegetable with meat
when boiled and buttered or creamed.   Chestnut purée with
sweetened whipped cream is an unusual and delicious dessert.
Blanched walnuts are particularly nice in making many dishes
and can be roasted with a little oil or butter and served hot and
crisp with meat.

CANNED AND PACKAGE GOODS FOR TWO

Although it is easy to feed a family of two with home cooked
fresh foods, as shown by the preceding suggestions, an acquaint-
ance with the possibilities of canned and packaged goods is
important to the manager of a very small household.   This is
particularly so in the case of one who does work outside her
home, or who makes her home in a kitchenette apartment where
space-saving is a major consideration.

Canned Vegetables eliminate the time-consuming operations of washing, scraping or paring, and simplify the problem of garbage disposal, which must always follow the preparation of fresh vegetables.

Fruits, Vegetables, Meats and Fish of many kinds come in cans of various sizes, so that it is possible to buy the size that experience teaches you is the best for your domicile.

Ready-to-Mix pie crust, pancake, cake and pastry flours shorten the time and reduce the utensils needed for mixing pies, biscuits, pancakes, muffins and cakes.

Fruits and Nuts in Cans or Jars of suitable size are always ready for salads, desserts, appetizers and garnishes.

Condensed, Evaporated and Powdered Milk may be kept in small space and, before they are opened, and if not kept too long, do not require a refrigerator temperature, as fresh milk does.

Steamed Puddings, pie-fillings, ready-to-mix pudding ingredients, canned welsh rabbit, chicken a la king, baked beans, spaghetti in savory sauces, soups of all varieties and countless other aids are at your service to help you serve varied and appetizing meals however limited your time or culinary space.

TYPES OF RECIPES ESPECIALLY SUITABLE FOR TWO

Appetizers

Soups

Broiled meats and fish

Shell fish

Soufflées

Croquettes

Patties

Creamed, scalloped and au gratin dishes

Cheese recipes

Egg dishes

Mushrooms in all ways

Entrées

Salads

Substantial sandwiches

Vegetables of all kinds

Quick breads

Fruit desserts

Gelatin and cream desserts

Cookies, gingerbread and small cakes

Tarts and turnovers

Recipes suggested in the chapter Cooking at the Table

COOKING AT THE TABLE

The small table cookers of various kinds—grills, chafing-dishes, waffle irons, muffin irons, pancake griddles, toasters and coffee percolators—make informal entertaining a pleasure to the hostess as well as to the guests.

Meals cooked at the table must of course be simple. It is usually wise to confine a supper to one hot dish, with such accessories as bread and butter, toast, crackers or cold sandwiches, a hot drink or a cold drink or both. If something more elaborate is desirable, the meal may begin with a fruit cocktail or a simple salad and end with a dessert that is easily served. Relishes, such as celery and olives, are easily provided.

SUGGESTIONS FOR TABLE COOKERY

It will help you to entertain successfully in this manner, if you will keep in mind the following suggestions:

1. Prepare Ahead of Time everything that can be prepared. Have the table spread with all that is needed in the way of china, silver and glass. Arrange the sandwiches, relishes and other cold accessories attractively and conveniently.

2. Have on Hand Everything That is to Be Used in the hot dish, and have it prepared as far as it is possible to prepare it. Meat or fish or vegetables should be nicely diced, cheese grated, oysters drained, and eggs broken into a bowl, unless they are to be cooked separately, as in poaching or frying. Lack of preparation often results in tiresome delays and unappetizing confusion, but with everything in readiness the one hot dish is easily put together before the guests become tired of watching the process.

3. Be Sure That Your Equipment Is Sufficient to provide for the needs of your guests. If you are giving a waffle party, do not invite more guests than your waffle iron will easily serve, so that no one need wait hungrily while others are eating. The same thing holds true with table grills and chafing-dishes. There should be enough creamed chicken or Welsh rabbit to serve everyone generously at the same time.

In the illustration is a croustade, filled with creamed chicken and fresh green peas.

With well selected equipment all the hot dishes of a simple meal may be cooked at the table. See page 204.

The very small family need not forego roasts of meat, as the little roasts above demonstrate. See page 199.

Vegetables as a rule are quite easily managed in the family of two. Suggestions will be found on page 200.

4. If Your Cookers Are Electric, be sure that your wires are heavy enough to bear the load without blowing out a fuse.

Unless you have special wiring and sturdy convenience outlets, it is safer not to attempt to use a grill or waffle iron plus a percolator on the same circuit. Plan to use first one and then the other, or you may melt a fuse when the meal is but half ready, leaving your guests hungry for that always indefinite period until it may be replaced.

Dishes That Are Especially Good for Table Cookery

BANANA SAUTE

1 tablespoon butter	Flour Sugar
3 bananas	3 to 6 slices sponge cake

Melt the butter in the blazer. Peel the bananas, cut in half lengthwise, roll lightly in flour and brown on both sides in the hot fat. Sprinkle with sugar and serve on oblongs of sponge cake.

CHICKEN HASH

1½ cups chopped chicken	1 tablespoon parsley
1 cup diced boiled potatoes	Salt Pepper
2 tablespoons fat	½ cup stock or water

Mix the chicken and the potatoes lightly together. Melt the fat in the blazer, add the potato and meat, parsley, seasoning and stock, and cook directly over the flame.

If desired, one-fourth cup of chopped green peppers may be added.

CRAB RABBIT

1 tablespoon fat	Pepper Parsley
2 tablespoons flour	1 to 2 cups crabmeat, fresh or
2 cups cream	canned
⅛ teaspoon soda	2 tablespoons Parmesan cheese
½ teaspoon salt	Toast

Make a white sauce of the fat, flour, cream, soda and seasonings. Add chopped cooked crabmeat. Arrange squares of buttered toast on a hot platter. Pour the crab mixture over them, sprinkle with grated cheese and serve piping hot.

ENGLISH MONKEY

1 cup bread-crumbs	1 egg
1 cup milk	½ teaspoon salt
1 tablespoon fat	¼ teaspoon pepper
½ cup mild American cheese	Toast

Soak the bread-crumbs in the milk until they are soft. Melt the fat in the blazer. Add the cheese cut in dice. When the cheese has melted, add the softened crumbs, the egg beaten, and salt and pepper. Cook three minutes longer and pour over squares of toast.

GRILLED SARDINES

12 large sardines   1 tablespoon lemon juice   6 pieces toast

Drain sardines and heat thoroughly in chafing-dish. Turn frequently; add lemon juice and serve on finger-length pieces of toast.

OYSTERS A L'INDIENNE

1 pint oysters	2 tablespoons Worcestershire
Bacon	sauce
Cloves	1 tablespoon minced parsley
2 tablespoons chutney	6 olives
sauce	½ teaspoon paprika

Drain large oysters, wipe them dry, wrap each in a slice of bacon, fastened with a toothpick, and stick two cloves in each oyster. Put the oysters in the blazer and cook until the bacon is crisp and the oysters plump. Mix the chutney sauce, Worcestershire sauce, minced parsley, olives cut fine, and paprika. Pour over the oysters, stirring it thoroughly into the gravy. This recipe will serve three or four.

PANNED OYSTERS

1 cup oysters	1 teaspoon parsley
1 tablespoon butter	Salt
White pepper	Toast
½ lemon	

Drain and wash the oysters. Put the fat in the pan and when hot turn in the oysters, adding the juice of the lemon and the chopped parsley. The oysters should be left only until they are plumped and the gills are a little ruffled. They must not change color, or be fried in the least. Season with salt and white pepper and serve on toast. This recipe will serve three.

LOBSTER A LA NEWBURG

2 tablespoons butter	1 pint milk
1 teaspoon flour	3 egg yolks
1 boiled lobster or 1 can	Salt
of lobster	Cayenne

Place the butter in the blazer and stir it as it foams. Rub the flour into the butter, add the salt and pepper, then one-half of the milk, stirring all of the time and being careful that the flame is not too hot. Beat the yolks of the eggs until frothy, add the remainder of the milk and stir into the roux. When the mass is of the consistency of cream, add the lobster, cut up coarsely, and, when thoroughly heated, serve. Just before adding the lobster, rub the coral and the fat together and stir in.

Other dishes that lend themselves to this form of entertaining, as well as to the family breakfast or supper, are:

Creamed Dishes — Creamed Chicken, Creamed Oysters, Chicken à la King, Tunafish with Caper Sauce, Oysters with Mushrooms, Creamed Sweetbreads, Creamed Mushrooms, Curried Dishes.

Hot Sandwiches—Grilled Cheese, Grilled Tongue and Egg, Club, Savory, Sardine and Toast.

Toast—Cinnamon, French.

Quick Breads—Griddle Cakes, Pancakes, Waffles.

Egg Dishes—Omelet (with any desired variation), Scrambled Eggs, Poached Eggs, Cuban Eggs, Spanish Eggs, Egg Fricassee.

Cheese Dishes—Welsh Rarebit, Cheese Fondue (on toast), Luncheon Cheese and Eggs.

Panned and Grilled Dishes—Panned Oysters, Little Pigs in Blankets, Rice Fan Tan, Fried Tomatoes, Hashed Brown Potatoes, Spanish Potatoes.

Candies — Fudge (in any variation), Butterscotch, Maple Scotch, Peanut Brittle.

FRENCH RECIPES

GREEN SOUP

2 bunches watercress	2 slices bread
2 diced potatoes	2 tablespoons butter
2 hard-cooked egg-yolks	

Cook the watercress until almost done, then add potatoes and cook until they are soft. Press through a sieve and add the purée to the water in which it was cooked. Brown the bread slightly in one tablespoon of the butter, and cut into small cubes. Add the minced egg-yolks and the remaining tablespoon of butter to the soup, season to taste, add the cubes of bread and serve hot.

CODFISH À LA BÉNÉDICTINE

1 pound fresh codfish	Butter
4 medium-sized sweet potatoes	Juice of 1 lemon
Salt	1 cup cream or milk
Pepper	Bread-crums

Boil the codfish, drain it and keep it warm.

Pare the sweet potatoes, cook them in salted water or steam them and let them dry, then mash and add a pinch of pepper, about two tablespoons of butter or butter substitute, the juice of half a lemon, and one cup of cream or milk.

Skin the fish and remove the bones. Pound it rather fine; add a tablespoon of butter and the juice of half a lemon. Mix the hot mashed potatoes with this. Add more milk or cream, so as to make a rough dough. Grease a baking-dish, and put the dough into it. Cover the top with bread-crums and melted butter. Put small dots of butter here and there on the top and bake in the oven for twenty minutes. Serve in the dish in which it was cooked.

CODFISH, BRANDADE STYLE

1 pound salt codfish
1 diced potato
2 tablespoons olive-oil

1 cup milk
Salt and pepper
3 tablespoons lemon-juice

Soak the codfish overnight, then put it in a saucepan of cold water, add the potato and cook on a quick fire. When it is on the point of boiling, remove it to the edge of the stove and cook on a slow fire, stirring constantly with a wooden spoon. Add the oil, drop by drop, and the milk. When it thickens it has been cooked long enough. Add the salt, pepper and lemon-juice, and serve hot.

CRABS WITH RICE

15 small crabs
1 cup rice
2 or 3 small onions

2 small carrots
1 tablespoon butter
Salt and pepper

Clean the crabs. Cut off and crush the legs, and cook in boiling salted water for about an hour. Strain the juice and pour it over the rice. Let stand for about half an hour and then cook until rice is tender. Cook the chopped onion and carrots in the butter until slightly browned and then add the crab-meat. Season with salt and pepper, add the rice and cook together for several minutes. Serve hot.

This is an old provincial recipe and has a particularly delicious taste that makes it a favorite.

FISH LOAF

2 cups cooked fish or 1 can fish
1 teaspoon salt

2 eggs
1 cup thick white sauce

Drain the fish and tear into small bits. Add the salt, the beaten egg-yolks, the white sauce, and the beaten egg-whites. Pour into a greased baking-dish and bake for twenty or thirty minutes.

SALMON À LA MORNAY

4 cooked potatoes
½ cup Swiss cheese
1 egg-yolk
Buttered crums

1 cup medium white sauce
2 cups boiled salmon or 1 can salmon

Mash the potatoes and line a greased baking-dish with them. Add the cheese and egg-yolk to the white sauce and pour half of it over the potatoes. Add the fish and cover it with the remaining sauce and buttered bread-crums. Bake in the oven for twenty minutes.

FISH EN COQUILLES

1 cup left-over fish
8 mussels or clams
½ cup bread-crums
10 tablespoons milk
1 clove garlic

1 teaspoon chopped parsley
1 chopped onion
Salt and pepper
3 tablespoons butter
Buttered crums

Chop the fish with the mussels or clams. Add the crums which have been soaked in two tablespoons of milk, and the garlic, parsley, onions, salt and pepper. Melt the butter or other fat, and when hot add the mixture and cook several minutes. Stir in one-half cup of milk and fill small ramekins or scallop shells. Cover with buttered crums and bake about fifteen minutes. Serve the dishes on a platter or on individual plates.

SAUSAGE WITH PEAS

8 pork sausages
1 tablespoon flour
½ cup water

½ cup peas
4 eggs

Cut the sausages in pieces about an inch long, and brown them in the frying-pan. When well browned, remove from the pan, pour off all the fat except one tablespoon, add to it the flour, and when browned, add the water. When the sauce is thick, put in the pieces of sausage, the peas, and beaten eggs. Pour into a baking-dish and bake in a slow oven until the eggs are set.

HAM LOAF

¼ pound lean ham
2 tablespoons flour
2 cups milk

¼ pound grated cheese
3 eggs
Salt and pepper

Cook the ham and chop it fine. Mix the flour with the milk and cook for a few minutes; then add the ham, cheese, the egg-yolks slightly beaten, and the stiffly beaten egg-whites. Season with salt and pepper, pour into a mold, set the mold in a pan of hot water and bake in a slow oven until firm. This may be served with or without a thin white sauce.

ECONOMICAL SAUCE FOR COLD MEAT AND FISH

4 tablespoons salad oil
4 tablespoons cream
3 tablespoons vinegar

Mustard
Salt
Pepper

Mix the salad oil, cream, vinegar, a little mustard, salt and pepper. Beat together quickly, with an egg-beater. The sauce gets white quickly and looks like whipped cream. Soon it becomes as thick as the best-made mayonnaise. Moreover, eggs are not required, the sauce will not curdle, and can be made quickly.

RED CABBAGE WITH CHESTNUTS

1 red cabbage
1 tablespoon drippings
½ cup melted grape jelly

½ cup water
Salt and pepper
French chestnuts

Select a nice red cabbage, remove the outer leaves and soak for a short time in cold water. Drain, and slice in thin shreds. Melt the fat in a saucepan, add the jelly and the cabbage, the water, salt and pepper. Cook very slowly until tender.

At the same time, boil some French chestnuts; take off the skin and add them to the cabbage. Cook all slowly for about two hours, until the liquid has evaporated.

STUFFED CABBAGE

1 cabbage
Butter or butter substitute
Parsley
Spices

1 cup bread-crumbs
3 eggs
1 chopped onion

Place a thin piece of cheese-cloth in the bottom of a bowl and lay the large cabbage leaves in it. Chop the middle of the cabbage fine and fry it in butter or butter substitute until it is yellow. Remove it from the fire, add a little chopped parsley, spices, bread-crums, eggs and onion. Place this mixture inside the large cabbage leaves, and tie up the cabbage by tying together the four corners of the cloth.

Place in a pan of boiling salted water and boil until the cabbage leaves are tender (about thirty-five minutes). When done, remove from the cloth, pour a little melted butter or butter substitute over it, and some fine bread-crums, and bake for five minutes. Serve with a tomato sauce.

EGGPLANT ORIENTAL

2 green peppers
2 eggplants
3 tablespoons cooking oil

6 ripe tomatoes
3 teaspoons salt
1 teaspoon paprika

Remove the seeds from the peppers, and cut the peppers into small pieces. Pare the eggplants and cut into small pieces. Cook the eggplant and peppers in the fat until slightly brown, then add the tomatoes and seasonings and continue the cooking until the eggplant is done. Serve very hot.

LIMA BEANS, NEUFCHÂTEL STYLE

2 cups green Lima beans or 1 cup dried Lima beans, soaked in water overnight
1 teaspoon salt

¼ cup butter
1½ cups milk
2 egg-yolks

Cook beans in boiling salted water until almost tender. Drain, remove skins and return to saucepan. Add fat, salt, and milk, and finish cooking. Just before serving, add slightly beaten egg-yolks diluted with a little milk.

MUSHROOMS AU GRATIN

½ pound mushrooms
1 sliced onion
2 tablespoons cooking oil
2 tablespoons flour
1 cup mushroom stock (made from stems)

½ cup bread-crums
1/16 teaspoon pepper
¼ teaspoon paprika
1 tablespoon butter
½ teaspoon salt
Juice of 1 lemon

Peel the mushrooms and sprinkle salt over them to extract the water. Fry the onion in the oil. Add the flour and brown; add the stock and seasonings and cook the sauce until it is thickened. Drain the mushrooms and add them to the sauce. Put into a baking-dish, sprinkle with crums and bake until the crums are slightly browned.

POTATOES, PEASANT STYLE

3 cups potatoes
6 tablespoons bacon fat
2 cloves garlic
2 tablespoons parsley
½ teaspoon paprika

2 tablespoons flour
2 cups milk
1 teaspoon salt
⅛ teaspoon pepper

Wash, pare and cut potatoes in dice. Fry in fat until brown. Remove potatoes and fry the chopped garlic and parsley in the fat remaining in the pan. Add flour, milk and seasonings, and cook until thickened (about five minutes). Add potatoes and cook three minutes.

SPINACH À LA REINE

½ tablespoon chopped onion
½ tablespoon butter
1 quart spinach
1 tablespoon flour
1 cup milk

Salt and pepper
3½ tablespoons grated cheese
3 eggs
6 cooked shrimps

Cook the onion in the butter or butter substitute, add the spinach, which has been washed and chopped, and fry quickly. Add flour and milk, and cook until it thickens. Season with salt and pepper, add grated cheese, and when it starts to boil remove from the fire and add well-beaten egg-whites, then the beaten yolks, and bake in a very hot oven for ten minutes. Garnish with the shrimps.

APPLES BAKED WITH BREAD

Remove the cores from good-sized apples; fill with jam and butter or butter substitute. Place round slices of stale bread in a baking-dish and put an apple on each. Pour scalded milk and water over the bread. Bake until the apples are soft. Serve in the baking-dish.

RICE CROWN WITH APRICOTS

Cook rice in milk and put in a buttered ring mold. When cool, turn into a fruit-dish. Cook dried apricots and place halves around the top of the crown. Strain the remainder of the fruit through a fine sieve and pour into the hollow of the crown. If this dish is desired hot, put the mold in the oven for a few minutes before trimming it with the apricots.

PRESERVES, MARMALADES, JAMS, CONSERVES AND FRUIT BUTTERS

CHERRY PRESERVES

2 pounds sour cherries, weighed   1½ pounds sugar
    after stoning

Add the sugar to the stoned cherries and bring them quickly to
the boiling-point. Cook rapidly until the fruit is clear, skimming
as necessary. Pour at once into clean hot jars and seal.

PEACH PRESERVES

Cling-stone peaches are better than free-stone, for they keep
their shape better. Wash, peel, and remove the stones if desired.
If the stones are removed, cut the peaches in quarters. Use
three-fourths pound of sugar, and three-fourths cup of water to
each pound of prepared fruit. Boil the sugar and water for ten
minutes. Skim, add the fruit and cook rapidly until it is transparent. Seal in clean hot jars.

RASPBERRY AND CURRANT JAM

1 pound red raspberries   ¼ cup currant-juice   ¾ pound sugar

Mash the fruit, add the currant-juice, and bring to the boiling-
point, stirring well from the bottom. Add the sugar and cook
until thick, stirring occasionally. Pack in clean hot jars and seal.

GREEN-TOMATO PRESERVE

8 pounds green tomatoes   1 tablespoon preserved ginger
6 pounds sugar   6 lemons

Wash the tomatoes, remove any dark parts about the stems, and
weigh them. Cover them with boiling water, let them stand five
minutes, drain and slice them into a preserving-kettle, placing a
layer of the tomatoes, then a layer of sliced lemon, then the sugar
with the ginger sprinkled over it. Let the mixture stand over-

night. Drain and boil the sirup for ten minutes. Skim, add the tomatoes and cook rapidly until they are clear. Pour into clean, hot jars and seal.

CARROT AND ORANGE MARMALADE

6 carrots	1 lemon
3 oranges	Sugar

Dice the carrots and cook them until they are tender, in as little water as possible. Cut the oranges in small pieces and add the juice and grated rind of the lemon. Measure the carrot and fruit, and add two-thirds as much sugar. Simmer the mixture until it is clear. Turn it into jelly glasses, and when it is cold, cover it with hot paraffin.

AMBER MARMALADE

1 grapefruit	$3\frac{1}{2}$ quarts water
1 orange	5 pounds sugar
1 lemon	

Wash and wipe the fruit. Cut in paper-thin slices, using a very sharp knife. Add the water and let stand overnight. Cook until the peel is tender and let it stand overnight. Add the sugar and cook until the sirup thickens slightly on a cold dish. Pour into clean jars and seal.

QUINCE AND APPLE MARMALADE

Wash the quinces and remove the blossom end. Cut the fruit in small pieces, add sufficient water to cover it, and cook until it is soft. Rub it through a sieve, and combine the pulp with an equal measure of tart apple pulp. Use two-thirds as much sugar as pulp. Cook until it is thick and clear (about twenty-five minutes). Turn it into clean, hot glasses and when it is cold cover it with hot paraffin.

CRANBERRY CONSERVE

2 quarts cranberries	2 lemons
1 cup raisins	6 cups sugar
2 oranges	

Combine the grated rind and juice of the oranges and lemons with the other ingredients and cook until the mixture is thick and clear. Pour into hot clean glasses and seal. This is an excellent relish with game.

CHERRY CONSERVE

3 pints pitted sour cherries   2⅔ cups sugar
1 pint black raspberries

Combine all the ingredients, and cook until thick and clear.

GRAPE CONSERVE

2 pints grapes   2⅔ cups sugar
2 oranges   1 cup walnut-meats
1 cup seeded raisins

Wash, stem, and seed the grapes. Slice the oranges very thin, and add to the grapes. Add the raisins and sugar and cook until the mixture is transparent and thick. Add the chopped walnut-meats. Pack while hot in hot, clean jars and seal.

MINT JELLY

Wash the mint and chop it fine. To each cup of chopped mint add one-fourth cup sugar and one-fourth cup water and let it stand overnight or for several hours. Place it over the heat and bring it to the boiling-point.

Make apple jelly, using two-thirds cup sugar to each cup of apple-juice. When the jelly test is observed, add green vegetable coloring and one or two tablespoons of the prepared mint for each quart of apple-juice.

SUGGESTIONS FOR CONSERVES, MARMALADES AND PRESERVES

1. One part peaches, three parts oranges, one part rhubarb, with nut-meats.
2. Equal parts peaches and plums, with nut-meats.
3. Two parts peaches, one part pineapple, one part rhubarb.
4. Equal parts peaches and apricots, with nut-meats.
5. Pears and ginger.
6. Two parts pears, one part orange, and one part pineapple.
7. Two pounds quinces, two oranges.
8. Equal parts grapes and crab apples, with nuts.
9. Equal parts plums and crab apples.
10. Apples with mint and nuts.
11. Two pounds figs, three pounds rhubarb, one lemon, one orange.
12. One part peaches, one part pineapple, one part white grapes with nuts.

PICKLES AND RELISHES

PICKLED NASTURTIUM SEEDS

Use green nasturtium seeds, and in picking retain a short length of stem on each. Lay the seeds in cold salted water for two days (two tablespoons salt to one quart water), then place them in cold water for another day. Drain well and place the seeds in a glass jar, cover with vinegar heated to the boiling-point, and close the jar tightly. In a few days the seeds will be ready to use. They are an excellent substitute for capers.

PEPPER MANGOES

Green peppers
Brine
1 quart chopped cabbage
1 tablespoon salt
1 tablespoon cloves
2 tablespoons white mustard seed
1 tablespoon cinnamon
1 cup sugar
Vinegar

Remove the stem ends of green peppers, carefully extract the seeds and midribs and lay the peppers in strongly salted water (one-half cup salt to two quarts water) for twenty-four hours. Chop the cabbage fine and add the salt, mustard seed, cloves, cinnamon and sugar, mixing them well. Drain the peppers, stuff them with the prepared cabbage, replace the pepper caps and tie them in position. Pack the peppers in a stone jar and cover them with strong cold vinegar. They will be ready to use in two or three weeks.

The amount of stuffing will need to be increased if many peppers are used. In increasing, keep the same proportions of ingredients.

GINGER PEARS

5 pounds hard pears
3 cups water
5 pounds sugar
1/3 cup preserved ginger
3 lemons, juice and grated rind

Remove the skin and cores from the pears and cut the fruit in slices lengthwise. Add the water and cook until the pears are tender. Add the sugar, juice and grated rind of the lemons, the ginger cut in small pieces, and simmer the mixture until it is thick. Pour into clean, hot jars and seal.

SPICED CURRANTS

4 quarts currants	1 teaspoon allspice
2 pounds white sugar	1 teaspoon cloves
1 pint vinegar	2 teaspoons cinnamon

Stem the fruit, and wash it. Make the sirup of the sugar, vinegar and spices and boil for five minutes. Add the fruit and cook until the mixture is thick and clear. Seal in clean, hot jars.

SPICED PLUMS

4 quarts plums	1 tablespoon ground cinnamon
3 pounds sugar	1 tablespoon cloves
1 pint vinegar	1 tablespoon allspice

Make a sirup from the vinegar, sugar and spices. Boil for five minutes. Prick each plum with a fork and pour the boiling sirup over the fruit. Let the whole stand three days, then skim out the plums, boil down the sirup until quite thick, add the plums and heat to boiling. Seal in clean, hot jars.

DIXIE RELISH

3 or 4 whole red peppers	1 pint white onions
1 pint chopped sweet green peppers	2 tablespoons salt
1 pint chopped sweet red peppers	4 tablespoons mustard seed
	2 tablespoons celery seed
1 quart chopped cabbage	3/4 cup sugar
	1 quart vinegar

Soak green and red peppers in brine for twenty-four hours, using one cup salt to one gallon water. Take from the brine and freshen in clear, cold water, from one to two hours. Drain well, cut open, remove seeds and white sections, and chop the peppers. Put cabbage and onions through the food-chopper separately and measure before mixing. Add chopped cabbage and onions to chopped peppers. Add salt, spices, sugar and vinegar. Let the mixture stand overnight in a covered crock or enameled vessel. Drain, and heat the liquid. When hot add the other ingredients and cook for ten minutes. Seal in clean, hot jars.

RED-PEPPER RELISH

12 red peppers	1 quart vinegar
12 green peppers	2 cups sugar
3 large onions	1½ tablespoons salt

Split the peppers and remove the seeds. Chop the peppers coarsely, pour boiling water over them and let stand for five minutes. Drain, pour more boiling water over them, and let stand ten minutes. Drain and add the chopped onions. Boil the vinegar, sugar, and salt for five minutes, and add all the other ingredients. Cook the mixture ten minutes after it has come to a boil. Pack in clean, hot glass jars.

BEET RELISH

1 quart chopped cabbage	2 cups vinegar
1 quart chopped cooked beets	1 cup sugar
1 cup grated horseradish	Salt

Combine the cabbage, beets and horseradish and season with salt. Scald the vinegar, dissolve the sugar in it and add it to the first mixture. Cook until clear. Seal in clean hot jars. This is particularly good with mutton.

CALIFORNIA CHOW-CHOW

18 green tomatoes	½ cup salt
8 cucumbers	2 quarts vinegar
5 dozen small green onions	1 cup brown sugar
1 pound green string-beans	2 tablespoons turmeric powder
1 cauliflower	4 tablespoons mustard seed
1 bunch celery	1 tablespoon cloves
3 chopped red peppers	1 tablespoon pepper

Dice the tomatoes, celery, and cucumbers, skin the onions and remove the tops, cut the beans in small pieces and separate the cauliflower into flowerets. Put all the vegetables, including the chopped red peppers, into an earthenware crock or bowl and sprinkle with the salt. Let stand twenty-four hours, then drain off the liquid. Heat the vinegar with the sugar and spices to the boiling-point, add the vegetables and cook until they are tender. Pack the pickles in clean, hot jars and seal.

CRANBERRY CATCHUP

2½ pounds cranberries
Vinegar
2⅔ cups sugar

1 tablespoon cinnamon
1 teaspoon ground cloves

Wash and pick over the cranberries. Cover them with vinegar and cook until they burst. Force through a sieve. Add the other ingredients, return the mixture to the fire and simmer until thick. Seal in clean, hot jars. Serve as a relish with fowl or meat.

GRAPE CATCHUP

4 pounds grapes
2 pounds sugar
1 pint vinegar

2 teaspoons cloves
2 teaspoons allspice
2 tablespoons cinnamon

Wash the grapes and remove them from the stems. Place them in a pan and steam them without water, until they are soft. Put the fruit through a sieve, add the other ingredients, and simmer the mixture for twenty minutes. Seal it in clean, hot jars.

OLD VIRGINIA CATCHUP

1 peck green tomatoes
½ peck white onions
3 ounces white mustard
   seed
1 ounce allspice
1 pound brown sugar

1 ounce cloves
½ cup dry mustard
¼ cup water
1 ounce black pepper
1 ounce celery seed
Vinegar

Chop the tomatoes and onions, sprinkle with salt, and let stand three hours. Drain well and put the pulp in a preserving-kettle with the other ingredients. Cover with vinegar, and boil slowly for one hour. Seal in clean, hot jars. Less mustard may be used if a less hot catchup is desired.